and the Bride Wore White

Seven Secrets to Sexual Purity

DANNAH GRESH

MOODY PRESS
CHICAGO

BOOK DESIGN BY JULIA RYAN

ISBN: 0-8024-8330-5

1   3   5   7   9   10   8   6   4   2

Printed in the United States of America

What young women are saying about

And the Bride Wore White:
Seven Secrets to Sexual Purity

"I don't know if I can fully explain what I experienced.
I got so much. It wasn't about abstinence. It was about life.
I met God truly for the first time."

LOLA, 16

"This book really spoke to my heart. I could not read it
without stopping again and again to pray or even to cry. I could
just really identify with what Dannah shared."

NYCOLE, 19

"It was phenomenal. We're watching the teaching spread like
wildfire on campus."

CARLA, A MENTOR IN A CHRISTIAN COLLEGIATE MINISTRY, 31

"My opinion is that it is one of the best I have ever read on
the topic. Our women desperately need this challenge."

DEAN OF WOMEN AT A CHRISTIAN COLLEGE

"This caused me to change my dating standards drastically.
I am now engaged and I know that this will have a lasting impact
on my marriage."

ERIN, 20

"I have learned about sex in a different way. Even after being
exposed to so much typical no-sex stuff, I just learned so much
more than I ever have."

MARIA, 14

To my princess, Lexi

*"All glorious is the
princess within her
chamber, her gown is
interwoven with gold.
In embroidered garments
she is led to the king."*

PSALM 45:13-14

CONTENTS

FOREWORD 9

ACKNOWLEDGMENTS 10

1 AND THE BRIDE WORE WHITE
Deciding to Live a Lifestyle of Purity...13

2 SATAN'S BIG FAT SEX LIES
Learning to Recognize the Truth..........19

3 SATAN'S BIGGEST, FATTEST SEX LIE
Resisting the Lure to Sin 27

4 SATAN'S SECOND BIG FAT SEX LIE
Hiding Behind the Fig Leaves.............35

5 BREAKIN' UP IS HARD TO DO
*Breaking Off Sinful Relationships
in Three Steps* 43

6 SECRET #1:
PURITY IS A PROCESS
Defining Innocence and Purity 53

7 SECRET #2:
PURITY DREAMS OF ITS FUTURE
Envisioning a Godly Husband 61

8 SECRET #3:
PURITY IS GOVERNED BY ITS VALUE
*Part A: Discovering Your Value
in God's Eyes*.....................................71

9 SECRET #3:
PURITY IS GOVERNED BY ITS VALUE
*Part B: Demonstrating Your Value
in the Eyes of Others*...........................81

10 SECRET #4:
PURITY SPEAKS BOLDLY
Preparing Your Tongue for Dates.........93

11 SECRET #5:
PURITY LOVES ITS
CREATOR AT ANY COST
*Pursuing a Love Relationship
with Jesus*...103

12 SECRET #6:
PURITY EMBRACES WISE GUIDANCE
*Inviting Your Parents into
Your Love Life*...................................113

13 THE TRUTH ABOUT SEX:
IT'S OUT OF THIS WORLD
*Understanding the Heavenly
Purpose of Sex* 125

14 THE TRUTH ABOUT SEX:
GETTING DOWN TO EARTH
*Preparing to Enjoy the Earthly
Gift of Sex* 133

15 NOT YOU AGAIN, SATAN!
*Facing the Consequences
to Find Healing* 141

16 SECRET #7:
PURITY WATCHES BURNING FLAMES
Finding M.O.R.E. to Help You........147

17 THE PAYMENTS ON THE
PEARL CONTINUE
*Using the Seven Secrets After Your
Wedding Day*..................................155

APPENDIX A: INTERVIEWS FROM THE HEART
*Five Christian Celebrities Talk About
Love, Sex, and Dating*.....................161

APPENDIX B: LETTERS FROM THE HEART
*Four Burning Flames Tell Their Stories
and Their Secrets*.............................172

FOREWORD:
A WORD FROM
JACI VELASQUEZ

It is so hard, in the world today, to keep a pure and holy mind when it comes to dating relationships. Everywhere you turn you're bombarded with models who have "perfect" bodies, relationships that are solely physical, and people who have no commitment values. As God's children, we are called to live with a higher standard; but how are we to have the strength to resist the many forces that we face? One way that has really helped me is to have one or two strong girlfriends whom I can confide in and who can help guide me. I'm lucky to have my mom as one of those friends. I think it's important to have a mentor who can share her experiences and wisdom from over the years. I hope that each one of you has a friend who can be a mentor in your life decisions.

The incredible thing about this book is that as you read and go through it, it feels like an intimate conversation with a close friend. Dannah talks openly about what she's gone through and what she's still struggling with even now that she's married. She reveals some of Satan's tactics to trick us into giving away the precious gift that God has given us. Dannah totally incorporates the truths that are in the Song of Solomon. She emphasizes the importance of not "arous[ing] or awaken[ing] love until it so desires" (Song of Songs 3:5), the value of approaching a relationship with caution and a guarded heart, and the blessings and pleasures that result from waiting.

I encourage you to completely and wholeheartedly dive into this book. I know it will be an encouragement for you as you stand strong in this world of pressure and confusion.

"Love does not delight in evil but rejoices with the truth"
(1 CORINTHIANS 13:6).

JACI

Acknowledgments:
The People in the Story Behind this Story

In August of 1997 the idea of writing a book on purity suddenly engulfed my every moment. My pride screamed for another assignment . . . a better (or perhaps safer) topic to write about. I designated one week to intense praying about it. I felt God's encouragement in many ways. At the very end of that week, a former employee walked up to me at an event and asked, "When are you gonna write that book I've always said you should write?"

That was it! The next day I told my husband and business partner, Bob, that he would just have to publish our monthly magazine, manage our marketing firm, and operate our radio station alone. I was going home to write a book. (Thank you, Sweetheart, for letting me do something so insane!)

By January, I had a proposal written. I couldn't imagine who would have the guts to rip it apart for me other than my dear friend and adviser from Cedarville College, Deb Haffey. Guess what? It just so happens that Deb had a close connection to Moody Press.

I now know that all the people at Moody, including Dennis Shere, Greg Thornton, and Jim Bell, moved things along at a rapid pace . . . but for a first-timer it seemed painfully slow. I found myself on the floor praying specifically that Moody would give me an answer by April 20. That very afternoon, Jim left a message on my machine explaining that he and the editorial staff at Moody would be meeting to make a final decision about my proposal on the morning of April 20! Wow! And the answer was, "Yes." Twelve weeks after I'd written the first proposal, I had a contract with Moody Press.

Oh, how wonderful, patient, and encouraging they have been with this impatient and sometimes overzealous first-time author. Bill Soderberg, managing editor, and Cheryl Dunlop, my editor, have kept me sounding intelligent. Dave DeWit and the others involved in the cover and internal design have allowed me the very rare privilege of having a voice in the final look of this book. (Isn't it beautiful? Thanks, Julia Ryan!) And everyone at Moody has been so good about giving Bob and me directions to the closest Chicago pizza restaurant. (Mmmmmm!)

Several close friends supplied some special support, from checks to pay for publicity to prayers to make it through long nights. Those friends include my brother Darin Barker, Tippy Duncan and her radical prayer club, Pastor Tim Cook, Rick and Ramona Taylor, Linda and Dan Goff, Tim and Kimberly Powers, Donna and Troy VanLiere, Marci and Sandi Hutchison, and Loretta Rodriguez.

Many young women who attended my sexual purity retreats while I was writing this book gave me great feedback and lots of wonderful encouragement. I am especially grateful to the girls from First Christian Church in Rolla, Missouri. A few of them—Nycole Flowers, Lauren Webb, Sarah Peaslee, Jennifer Goble, Jennifer Rodriguez, Shantelle Russell, and Jennifer Vogel—appear as the models on the cover and within this book. Antoinette and Randy Moore, Heather Goble, little Kristine Breshears, Stephanie Pritchette, Louis Rodriquez, and Brian Rapier also posed for my talented photographer, Dan Seifert. Jaci Velasquez and Mike Atkins Management and True Love Waits have been so generous to lend their support and credibility to this project.

Finally, I just have to tell you about how my family has been involved. My sweet son Robby, who is nine as we go to press, was and is my biggest fan, even though he cannot read this book until he is a teenager. My mom and dad are very much reflected in this work. Their examples continue to mold me and inspire me. (And writing the bulk of this book in their mountain cabin was fun, even if I never saw the black bear they brag so much about!) My husband, Bob, has decided that he believes in this project as much as I do. He has also "left" our three thriving businesses to manage and market this little book of mine. More important, he continues to work with me so that our marriage will model the love of Jesus Christ for His church. And that is what this book is really all about . . . Jesus and His love. If you see His love within these pages, I will be most honored. Thank You, my Jesus, for loving me and for making me pure!

Dannah

deciding

to live a

lifestyle of

purity

AND THE
BRIDE WORE
WHITE

Deciding to Live a Lifestyle of Purity

*[God's grace] teaches us to say "No" to ungodliness
and worldly passions, and to live self-controlled,
upright and godly lives in this present age, while we
wait for the blessed hope—the glorious appearing of
our great God and Savior, Jesus Christ.*
(TITUS 2:12-13)

 *The day I met the man who would become my husband* he had just returned from Florida, where he and the rest of the varsity tennis team had spent spring break practicing endlessly. His white teeth contrasted sharply with the deep tan and his dark hair. His nose was peeling just a bit as he began to flirt with me. That profile of his cheery countenance is etched in my mind forever.

On my wedding day and at my request, his tan was there to contrast with the clean white shirt and bow tie we had chosen for him to wear under his long black tails. He was the man of my dreams, and this day was a fairy tale come true. And me? I wore a white hand-beaded dress with a nine-foot train and a sequined tiara veil. I marched across fresh rose petals as violinists, stretched along both sides of the sanctuary, played the wedding march. At the front of the sanctuary, we faced our guests so that they could see the joy on our faces as we exchanged vows. The kiss was sweet and simple, ending with a knowing glance. There would be more time for tenderness that night.

At the reception, guests munched on hors d'oeuvres as an orchestra played in the background, pausing only for the announcement from the master of ceremonies, "Ladies and Gentlemen, our bride and groom have arrived. I present for the first time in public Mr. and Mrs. . . ." I was a Mrs.! Applause filled the room as the strains from the orchestra ushered us to our head table. I waltzed beautifully with my father, who returned a bow to my groom a few minutes into the waltz. As my new husband and I started to dance, we succeeded in royally ruining the graceful presence my father had established, but it didn't matter. We were the prince and princess of the ball, and anything we did would charm the guests.

Hours later, the princess found herself locked in the bathroom of a honeymoon suite trying to decide how to make her grand entrance. (If I had it to do over again, I would claim the room for myself and lock *him* in the bathroom to decide when and how to enter!) Was it too soon for the lacy negligee? Were the full-length satin pj's too modest for tonight? Should I put my hair up? Would it seem too vain to freshen my makeup? We had not discussed lights—would they be on or off when I came out? In the end, I opted for the modesty and the vanity. (And hoped the lights would be low!)

But when my eyes met my husband's deep blue ones . . . full of compassion and true love . . . the nervousness was replaced with a knowing. We had waited. We had made it through the maze of temptation, and now a warm and comforting Presence was with us, assuring us that this covenant into which we were about to enter would be blessed.

And the blessing was more than we had hoped for.

—————— ❧❦ ——————

How did we make it? God knows that I was not perfect. How did I wait for the wonderful gift of being one with a man I so tenderly loved? Well, it's a wonderful, romantic story that includes moments of critical decisions . . . some I am proud of and some I wish I had made differently. I am going to share it all with you. Through it I learned seven special secrets that gave me the strength to make it through a lot of temptation.

It all started with the truth of Titus 2:12-13. Those verses say that God's grace does not automatically keep us from worldly passions. In all of your love for God, you could be blindsided by worldly passions. When I realized how difficult the path of purity can be, I stood before God and I said, "OK, teach me to say no. I know these worldly passions exist, but I know the only way I will be able to say no is if You teach me!" And from that moment on, God worked in me and gave me a resolve that I did not even know that I could have within me. The path . . . and the waiting . . . were much easier. The difference was that now I had placed myself in God's presence to be taught how to say no to worldly passions.

If you didn't go to class, your teacher could not fill you with all of the knowledge that he or she had to give. The God of the universe won't teach you either, unless you place yourself in His presence. I have been praying for you. I want so desperately for you to stand before God and to ask Him to teach you to say no to worldly passions so that you can live a self-controlled, godly, upright life.

You cannot attain purity all on your own.

I cannot unveil to you some formula of protection.

Your parents cannot tell you something that will keep you innocent.

Only God can do that!

Won't you stop right now and ask Him to teach you as you read this book to say no to worldly passions?

Write Your Story

Now, here is the most important part of this book. You need a journal or notebook to really make this book change your life. You see, it's not what I write that is important and can protect your purity. It is what you write that will knock Satan between the eyes.

it's your **turn**

Get out your journal and write a letter to God. Explain to Him where you are in your struggle to stand pure before Him. It could be any area of your life–sexuality, substance abuse, language, anger–anything that is causing heartache in your life. Give each part of your history over to Him. Tell Him you are sorry if you have failed. Pray that He will keep you shielded from worldly passions. And specifically request Him to be your teacher while you are reading this book.

Go ahead. Write!

I have prayed for you and for this very moment in your life.

If you feel God telling you to ponder what you've written or what you have heard Him saying, then just be quiet for today, but come back soon! You and I are going on a complete journey of our sexual lives–that is, yours and mine. For me, we're going to go back a few years, and I am going to tell you about some of my most intimate moments–some shameful and some quite beautiful. For you, we are going to build a complete godly vision of your love life to come. Let's go!

you will soon see, not every choice I made about my sexual purity was governed by God's plan. I never dreamed of having a ministry to encourage young girls to treasure their purity. God pushed me into doing my very first purity retreat when a conflict arose in my church over whether or not a junior in high school should attend a women's retreat dealing with sexual healing.

Since I was a corporate trainer, the women of the church asked me to put together a purity retreat specifically for the junior and senior high girls. I have to admit, my pride pleaded with the Lord for another assignment, but I eventually gave in. I did not share any of myself on that first retreat, but I saw women who did, and I saw how incredible the response was to how "real" they were. I cautiously walked into the arena of exposing myself and found junior high, senior high, and college-aged girls who were incredibly challenged by my story, much to my humility. It made them eager to explore God's heart on the matter of sexuality. And so, I offer you my story in these pages. It has been rewritten through meticulous retrieval of my memory through sixteen years of diaries and journals. I present it in a narrative format at the beginning of each chapter. Not one detail written about within these pages was made up. They were all carefully recorded within my journals. God must have known they would be used for this book.

My Friends' Stories

Laced throughout this book are many short stories about friends I have known for years or have met at my purity retreats. Not one of these stories is made up either. In many cases, I use just a first name or I have changed the name to protect the person's privacy or the privacy of someone else who may have been involved in the person's story.

CHAPTER TWO

learning to

recognize

the truth

SATAN'S
BIG FAT
SEX LIES

Learning to Recognize the Truth

*The devil . . . was a murderer from the beginning,
not holding to the truth, for there is no truth in him.
When he lies, he speaks his native language,
for he is a liar and the father of lies.*
(JOHN 8:44)

Hot, thick air engulfed the camp where I had gathered with dozens of other Christian teens to be trained as a "summer missionary." We would be spending the summer teaching Bible classes in underprivileged neighborhoods. We eagerly dug into stacks of visual aids and endless pages of mandated Bible stories, hoping to impress our teachers, who would rigidly scrutinize our delivery and memorization.

Laying my chin down on the picnic table, I pondered the others studying among the trees.

Good thing I'm not lookin' for guys here, I thought, reflecting again on the near absence of them. *Anyway, I've got the greatest guy of all waiting for me at home.*

I reached into my pocket for the letter, which I'd already read a dozen times. I hoped another letter would come today. As if God were monitoring my distracted devotion, thunder rumbled in the distance.

Moments later, the clouds burst suddenly and quickly flooded the tiny stream that ran through the camp. Dozens of us frolicked and romped in the water up to our hips. We played football, tackled one another, and floated in the gentle current as the fresh June rain poured onto the ground and into our spirits.

When the sun authoritatively returned, our soggy clothes suddenly weighed us down, and we gave in to the cries of our sponsors to come inside. As I stepped onto the dorm steps, Jenny gasped. I looked at her with a raised eyebrow.

"You're bleeding," she said, pointing to my foot.

Lifting my foot, I could see a small piece of glistening glass.

"Doesn't hurt," I assured my tenderhearted friend as I pulled the glass from my foot.

Within hours, I had a red line climbing my leg—the beginning of blood poisoning. Much like an undiagnosed, growing deadly cancer, it did not hurt. I spent the next twenty-four hours soaking my wound to extract the poison.

I did not know it at the time, but that day would be a portrait of the next few years of my life. Those years would prove that the most blissful moments often have deadly potential—even if it doesn't hurt at first.

———— ❧❦ ————

I was channel surfing and was stopped dead in my tracks by a program called "Guys and Sex." It was a string of interviews with young men talking about sex. I was intrigued. I have often wanted to get into the heads of guys to see what they were really thinking.

Two handsome brothers seemed to be the hunks and sexual bravadoes of the program. Their shoulder length, wavy hair gave them a sort of Fabian look. They spent the nights prowling for women. Their goal? To have a new "lover" every evening. And with their looks and charm, they did.

They talked of their conquests with laughter and freedom. They were having fun. But the last take was what intrigued me.

As they sat in a hot tub sipping beers, the interviewer asked, "Do you think you'll every marry?"

The brothers laughed. "Yeah, whatever," said one.

"Doesn't everyone?" boasted the other.

"But, seriously," pushed the interviewer, "will you marry?"

The laughter stopped. One set his beer down and ran his fingers through his hair nervously. He then looked pensively into the distance.

"Yeah, but not for a long time," he said.

"Who will you marry?" asked the interviewer.

"Not any of these girls," he spoke with assurance. "I want my wife to be pure."

———— ❧❦ ————

The beauty of sexual love is being camouflaged by big fat lies. That, of course, is because Satan has entered onto the scene. John 8:44 tells us the true character of Satan. The devil "was a murderer from the beginning, not holding to the truth, for there is no truth in him. When he lies, he speaks his native language, for he is a liar and the father of lies." What is Satan? He is a big fat liar. And I think his favorite lies relate to your sexuality because of its powerful symbolism. (We will talk more about that later. For now, know that the true meaning of sex is so far beyond the pitiful meaning this world offers that it'll blow your mind if you've never heard about it!)

I like to compare the way he lies to you and me about sex to the way he lied to Eve about the Tree of the Knowledge of Good and Evil. Why? God's Word tells us that everything in the Garden of Eden was created by God's own hand. It also tells us that He is incapable of making anything that is not good. So, it is very possible that the Tree of the Knowledge of Good and Evil would have had quite an interesting and noble purpose had Eve simply *waited* for God to reveal it to her in His time. Interesting thought, don't you think? My friend, sex is like that. It is such a good and wonderful thing that God has created *if we wait* for God's timing to enjoy it. Satan knows that one of the most beautiful things in our world is the sexual union between a husband and a wife when they wait to enjoy it after their wedding. He wants to rob you of that, so he lies to you.

"teach me to say no"

I think he told those brothers on TV that it would give them power and fulfillment. But you can tell that deep down they have some sense of the deception. Why else would they need so many conquests?

He told my friend Aimee that a sexual relationship with her boyfriend could heal the pain she felt from not having a good relationship with her dad.

He told my Christian friend Jennifer that she would lose her boyfriend if she did not provide for some of his sexual needs—though she told him she would not have sex with him. He raped her.

He told my Christian friend Leeza that if she did everything but actual intercourse, she was still "pure."

When I was fifteen, he told me that I was protected in a strong Christian dating relationship. I did not feel that I needed to be watchful. I lost a great deal of my innocence through that deception.

One of Satan's lines is "everyone is doing it." What a lie! Everyone is not doing it. In *The Glory of Sex,* Edwin Louis Cole refers to a survey of one thousand teenagers. The study found that "fifty percent had admitted that they had already engaged in sex while still in high school."[1] That leaves 50 percent who hadn't!

Here's another big fat lie. Satan decided there were not enough teenagers sacrificing their innocence, so he came up with a grand scheme. He got their parents to think, *If everyone is doing it, and there is something awful like AIDS out there, I had better give my kids tools to do it safely.* Now he has parents and mentors saying, "Have safe sex!"

Satan's lie is that to keep you safe, we have to teach "safer sex." The truth is that most teenagers are saying that they don't want to hear it,[2] and it really isn't safe at all. Safe sex is one of the most dangerous activities that exist. Condoms, the armor of the safe-sex mentality, provide little protection against sexually transmitted diseases.

The human papilloma virus (HPV) is the most common viral STD, causing more than 2.5 million new infections each year. HPV is incurable, uncomfortable, and gross–it causes genital warts–but more important it causes more than 90 percent of all cervical cancer.[3] Guess how much protection a condom provides against HPV? None. How safe is that? It simply isn't safe at all.

You probably know that. Many of you are becoming more vocal about opposing the safer sex message. Kristine Napier, author of *The Power of Abstinence*, a book written from a completely nonreligious point of view, writes:

Sixty-three percent of teens surveyed by a USA Today survey said they didn't want to hear the safe sex message, believing that it endorses casual sex. Similarly, a 1986 Planned Parenthood/Harris Poll found that the majority of teens mistrusted the safe sex message, saying it actually encouraged them to be unusually active. In that same survey, an astonishing 87 percent of teens said they did not want comprehensive sexuality services in their schools.[4]

Know this, friend! Satan looks at your sexuality much like he did Eve's Tree of the Knowledge of Good and Evil. He is threatened by it and will do anything to see that you misuse it.

Of course, Satan uses many lies, and he customizes them each time to be just right for the person to whom he is lying. But as I listen to women tell their stories about their road to purity, I hear three distinct lies that Satan tends to use. They are much like the lies he told Eve in the garden. I want you to know what they are so you can see them when he throws them your way. Here comes the first of Satan's biggies!

Write Your Story

What do you think? How has Satan deceived you? Wait! 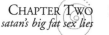 Before you think that you have not been deceived, think about it for a moment. Ask God to reveal to you anything of which you  might not be aware. (I was not aware of my deception. It was a clever one!) Even if you hold strongly to your innocence and you desire to walk down the wedding aisle innocent, pray that God would reveal to you what part in your heart needs to be challenged and purified. This is very important. Take time to write your search and your prayer out to the Lord in your journal.

NOTES

1. Edwin Louis Cole, *The Glory of Sex* (Tulsa: Honor Books, 1993), 34.
2. Kristine Napier, *The Power of Abstinence* (New York: Avon Books, 1996), 73.
3. House of Representatives, Representative Tom Coburn of Oklahoma, "Sexual Health Today: Exploring the Past, Preserving the Future Through Choices Today," a slide presentation provided by the Medical Institute of Austin, Tex. *Congressional Record* (17 September 1998), H8022.
4. Napier, *Power of Abstinence,* 73.

CHAPTER THREE

resisting

the lure

to sin

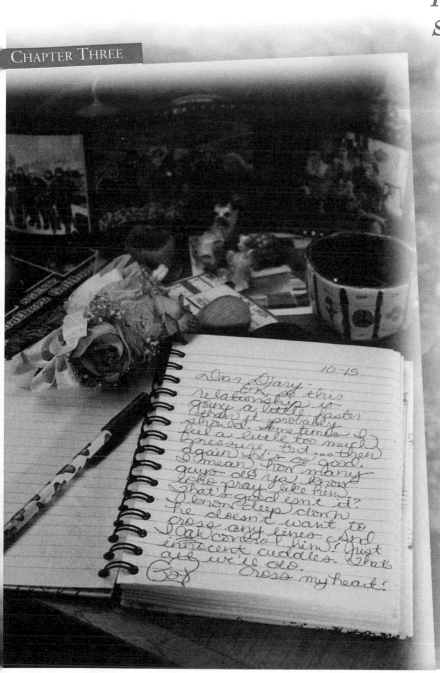

10-15

Dear Diary—
OK, so this
relationship is
going a little faster
than it probably
should. Sometimes I
feel a little too much
pressure, but ...then
again, it's so good.
I mean, how many
guys do ya know
who pray like him.
That's good isn't it?
I know deep down
he doesn't want to
cross any lines. And
I can control him! Just
innocent cuddles. That's
all we'll do.
Cross my heart!

SATAN'S BIGGEST, FATTEST SEX LIE

Resisting the Lure to Sin

"Hey! Don't you know God is withholding a good thing from you?"

1 Now the snake was the best liar of all the animals that God had made. He said to Eve, "Hey, did I hear God say, 'You can't eat from any trees in the garden'?" 2 Eve answered, "Oh, we can eat from the trees in the garden 3 but God did say 'You must not eat from that tree in the middle of the garden. Don't even touch it or you will die.'" 4 "Oh, you won't die," lied the snake. 5 "Come now, God knows that when you bite into that fruit you will be so full of knowledge. Why, you'll be just like God, knowing good from evil." 6 So Eve looked at the tree and noticed that it was full of fruit and beautiful. Suddenly she believed it would give her wisdom. So she took some and ate it. She also gave some to Adam, who was standing right beside her, and he ate it.

(GENESIS 3:1-6, AUTHOR'S PARAPHRASE)

I sat dazed in the corner of the classroom. The recruiter who had encouraged me to be a summer missionary the previous summer was here to tell the junior class at my Christian high school about being a summer missionary.

As she began to talk, my mind wandered off to the previous June, to summer missionary camp. I was walking down the concrete camp pathway. I joined the circle of other new graduates, and we sang, "I've got joy, down in my heart . . . deep, deep down in my heart! J-O-Y down in my heart." I did have joy. My love for Jesus was so intense that it gave me butterflies to think of the little children who awaited my Bible stories that summer.

Over the summer, dozens of young lives placed their hearts in Jesus' hands. Every Wednesday, I was true to the contract that I had signed as I spent a minimum of one full hour in prayer for my ministry and the ministry of the other summer missionaries. Sometimes I grabbed the phone and called one of them. We were so close. God had developed an awesome bond of friendship between us. Once, one of the neatest guys at the camp called me . . . and we prayed over the phone for each other's ministry and for God's protection . . . zzzzzzzrip . . .

I was on another path, and I wasn't feeling protected. It was October and I was walking down a pathway in the woods with Michael. We were alone. I wanted to be with him, and yet I didn't. The past few months had been a labyrinth of temptation, and I could not find the way out. His desires were ones I could not identify with as he groped and grabbed at me every chance he had. I was like a deer in oncoming headlights. I did not know how to respond. I wanted him to stop forcing his desires upon me, yet they had awakened other desires within me. I wanted to belong to him and to be wanted by him. Whenever he'd write to me—oh, those letters wove webs around my heart. And he always expressed so much of a desire to serve God together. I mean, look at him—he is good, and he is good for me. I could control him. Kisses, cuddles . . . just innocent touching. I could control him. But at the end of that path I found how very out of control I was . . . zzzzzrip.

"Dannah was a summer missionary last summer and is going to share some of her experiences with you," my recruiter said, ripping me back into the room. She also brought me back into the miserable reality that I had forfeited what really was a good thing for something that only looked like a good thing, but that had turned out to be a lonely, imprisoning act of sin.

If you didn't read all of Genesis 3:1-6 (on the previous page) because you know the story, go back and read it again.

Verses 4 and 5 are where Satan dealt a literal deathblow to Eve. Notice how he first appealed to her intellect, making her feel inferior by saying, "Oh, you won't die . . . come now, don't *you* know that God knows you will be just like Him when you bite into that fruit?" He talked as if he had experience. Do you know what I think? I think that even Satan, like Adam and Eve, knew nothing of what death meant. After all, when would he have seen it? I think only God knew what the full consequences would be.

Satan was basically saying, "Hey, don't you know God is withholding something good from you? I know how truly good it is and that it really won't hurt you at all but will make you just like God."

He caused Eve to believe that she had the intellect to draw her own moral-ity—or to determine what was right for her. Oh, if only Eve had stood firmly on the truth of what God said. He said, "Of the tree of the knowledge of good and evil *you shall not eat,* for in the day that you eat of it you shall surely die" (Genesis 2:17 NKJV, italics added). God said no, and Eve should have too. Instead, she decided she was smart enough to debate the devil. And because Eve was busy talking, he found her weakness . . . touch. She had told him God said they couldn't even touch it. Perhaps that gave him an idea. "Oh, you won't die," hissed the snake as he slithered around the ripe fruit, tempting her to reach out to "just" touch it.

"just touch it"

Today, Satan still loves to make you feel inferior, like you are missing some-thing and can't measure up. He likes to make you think that you cannot possi-bly wait for this wonderful gift and that if you're really intelligent about it, you shouldn't have to wait. Eve's story sounds so much like the sexually enlightened world in which you and I live. We're constantly being thrust into debate over sexual issues. But, as Ed Young reminds us in *Pure Sex,* "All that the current experts have managed to give us in terms of sexual enlightenment has not sat-isfied our longing for something transcendent, something pure and beautiful. Instead, we've settled for what some have called 'nutra-sex'—artificial substi-tutes for pure sex that eventually cause cancer—both in relationships and in the soul."[1]

Oh please, stand firm . . . firm . . . firm on God's Word. Ephesians 5:3 says that within the church, "There must not be even a hint of sexual immorality, or of any kind of impurity." Paul says, "But not everything is good for us. So refuse to let anything have power over you. Don't be immoral in matters of sex. That is a sin against your own body *in a way that no other sin is*" (see 1 Corinthians 6:12, 18).

God says "No!" and you can too! No debating. Just "No!"

Sometimes, if you have enough resolve, Satan whispers into your ear, "You don't have to go all the way. Just try a few little things. That won't hurt."

Oh, no! Here comes that "touch" again. It seems Eve is not the only female to throw that into the debate.

I told you before that my friend Leeza believed the lie that if she just did not have intercourse she would be pure. Leeza was one of the most gorgeous girls I have ever known. Her hair was long and a natural rich chestnut color. Her facial features were dainty. She was a catch, and the guys knew it. She dated anyone, but leaned toward the athletic playboys. They would date her for awhile, get as much as they could from her sexually, and then drop her because it wasn't enough. So she really got around.

Toward the end of our college years, Leeza really began to regret her lifestyle. She realized that she now had a reputation that would follow her the rest of her life. It would be difficult to return to her tiny hometown without running into a guy who had a sexual memory of her.

> "There is a dullness, monotony, sheer boredom in all of life when virginity and purity are no longer protected and prized. By trying to grab fulfillment everywhere, we find it nowhere."
>
> ELISABETH ELLIOT,
> PASSION AND PURITY[3]

In my last few years of college, I saw a lot of friends who had guarded their virginity through the toughest years suddenly give in to testing their sexual performances right before their wedding or even before they became engaged. Most of them were remorseful of their choice. Several got pregnant.

Regretfully, my own innocent "touching" gradually escalated into a form of "nutra-sex." I can tell you that it left a painful cancer that I thought might never be cured. I fell for Satan's lie that God was withholding something really great from me.

God's truth is that there is a reason to wait. A study by Tim and Beverly LaHaye found that married women who had no premarital sexual experience were about 10 percent more likely to be sexually satisfied in their marriage than those women who had lost their virginity before their wedding day.[2]

Guess what? God's Word promises that very thing in Deuteronomy 6:24 when it says, "The Lord commanded us to obey all these decrees . . . so that we might always PROSPER!" The writer was talking about the laws God had just given. He was explaining that the purpose of them was to make the nation of Israel prosperous. I see that trend throughout Scripture. God desired for Israel then, and He desires for you and me today, to live strong, healthy, prosperous lives. God does not withhold anything from us to frustrate us. He knows how much more glorious sex will be if we wait. Let me say this one more time. God says "No!" and you can too. No debating. No touching. Just "No!"

I'll tell you a few more secrets about prospering in God's truth later on. First, I have to tell you about the second big lie and how I fell for it, because the first one and the second one usually hit hard and fast. You cannot fully understand the impact of the first without understanding the sting of the second.

NOTES
1. Ed Young, *Pure Sex* (Sisters, Oreg.: Multnomah, 1997), 12–13.
2. Tim and Beverly LaHaye, *The Act of Marriage* (Grand Rapids: Zondervan, 1976), 210.
3. Elisabeth Elliot, *Passion and Purity* (Grand Rapids: Revell, 1984), 21.

SATAN'S
SECOND
BIG FAT
SEX LIE

CHAPTER FOUR

hiding

behind

the fig

leaves

SATAN'S SECOND
BIG FAT SEX LIE

Hiding Behind the Fig Leaves

"Ha! Now that you've fallen, God has no use for you!"

*7 Then Adam and Eve suddenly realized they were naked and
they sewed fig leaves together to cover themselves. 8 Then the
man and his wife heard the sound of God walking nearby in the
garden in the cool of the day, and they hid behind some trees.
9 And God called to Adam, "Where are you?" 10 He answered,
"I heard You and I was afraid because I was naked, so I hid."
11 God said, "Who told you that you were naked? Have you
eaten from the tree I told you not to?" 12 Adam said, "It was the
woman You gave me. She gave some to me, and I ate it."
13 Then God said to Eve, "What have you done?" Eve answered,
"It was the snake. He deceived me and I ate it."*

(GENESIS 3:7-13, AUTHOR'S PARAPHRASE)

Each night was the same. I walked along a dark, busy
highway with Michael. Horns blared. Lights glared, and yet the
darkness was thick. Aside from the busy highway, I couldn't see
anything but blackness.

I held my boyfriend's hand more tightly. I turned to look at
him. I called his name.

He quickly looked away, avoiding my gaze. I called him again.
Why wouldn't he look at me?

Suddenly a great shaft of light dropped from the sky and loomed authoritatively in front of us. It had a warm golden glow, which contrasted sharply
against the coldness of the rest of this place. My boyfriend quietly pulled his
hand from mine, and I felt him step behind me. The great light was directly in
front of me.

I did not hear a voice, but I felt as if that shaft of light was the presence of
God inviting me to step into it—to choose God instead of this earthly love that
I wanted to turn and cling to. I hesitated just long enough for the light to vanish

as quickly as it appeared. I turned around, and my boyfriend was gone.

The highway was empty.

The darkness engulfed me.

I was alone.

"No!" I screamed, waking from my deep sleep.

Blue moonlight reached into my bedroom and created a shaft of light across my bed. I looked into it and scrunched deeper into the blankets, heavy with a cold sweat.

How many times in the past months had that dream awakened me from my restful slumber? It was like no other dream I had ever had. It was real, and every detail was memorable. There was meaning in it. My pain was so great.

I inched deeper and deeper into the covers and hid in my cold sweat.

The man who is now my wonderful husband was a resident assistant in college. Once he walked into a unit to check on things late Saturday evening. He heard weeping coming from a closet. Opening the door, he found a guy curled up in the closet. The young man wanted to be left alone in that closet, but he was an emotional wreck.

After lengthy consolation and trying to determine what could possibly have driven a healthy, strong man to hide in his closet and wail, an admission came. The young woman he had been dating and hoped to marry one day had finally agreed to have sex with him. They did. And now he was hiding, uncertain as to whether or not he could repair the disrespect he had shown her and himself.

Sound familiar? Sort of like what Adam and Eve did after they bit into that fruit. Oh, my friend, I can tell you that they did not hide lightly. They hid with a great sense of grief and guilt. I know from experience.

In choosing my boyfriend I lost the awareness of the very presence of God that I once so loved. It was a lot like Adam and Eve's experience. It wasn't that God wasn't there. He was walking nearby saying, "Where are you, Dannah?" I was too ashamed to come out. I resigned from teaching Sunday school. I quit my job as a summer missionary.

I hid.

I can just see Satan off in the corner laughing, "Ha! Now that you've fallen, God has no use for you!" It took me a very long time to realize that was a big fat lie! (Oh, to have those years back!)

What's the truth?

Before I get to the bottom line, let me first say there is no escaping the consequences of sin. Adam and Eve, because of their sin, were kicked out of the garden. Adam had to work hard to feed his family, and Eve would experience great pain in childbirth. Even the snake lost his legs. The consequences were tough.

King David truly sinned—he had sex with another man's wife (Bathsheba). Then, because he got her pregnant, he ended up killing her husband to hide his sin. Some pretty tough consequences, really. There's an illegitimate baby on the way and blood on David's hands. I bet David and Bathsheba both had a lot of sleepless nights. I can picture Bathsheba greatly mourning the loss of her husband's life because, in a way, it was her fault. And later when the child died, I can see them both thinking about the fact that they would never have known that horrible loss had they not sinned together.

Yes, the consequences of sin can last a long time and be very painful, *but does that mean that God no longer wanted David to be in a loving, lasting relationship with Him?* Well, God watched the whole soap-opera-like drama unfold, and He sent Nathan to confront David. (My guess is that David was in the place where you think you have to work your way back into God's heart—wipe the slate clean and *then* come before God.) When David was confronted, he repented, and Nathan immediately said, "The Lord has taken away your sin" (2 Samuel 12:13). There was no hesitance, no delay. God immediately welcomed David back into His presence. And He did continue to use him. David will forever be honored as "a man after God's own heart!" (*see* 1 Samuel 13:14).

Did his sexual sin mean that God had no use for him? No!

Satan likes to make you feel as if your sin has ruined you and will stick with you forever. The truth is that God picks up that sin and hurls it as far as the east is from the west. He promises us in Ezekiel 18:22 that "none of the offenses he has committed will be remembered." Believe that. Know the truth of God. And crush Satan's lie with it.

For a long time I felt as if my sexual sin was my ultimate destruction. I had forsaken God's plan and made a lesser choice. My heart got tangled up, and now I was paying the consequences. I felt lonely in the midst of what should have been a fun relationship. I felt trapped during years when I should have been feeling free and enjoying my singleness. I felt ashamed to enter into God's presence.

Ever *feel* something like that? Yours may not be necessarily sexual in nature. Maybe you are just *consumed* with the idea of having a boyfriend. Or your language robs you of your testimony. How do you release it so that you don't feel utterly useless in God's hands or useless in general?

Let me try to bring the classic writing of the great author C. S. Lewis into today's lingo. In *The Great Divorce,* he writes about a slimy red lizard clinging to a certain ghost. The lizard taunted and teased that ghost, whispering great lies to him every day. The ghost tried to control the lizard, but it was not successful.

An angel appeared and offered to rid the ghost of the little lizard. But the ghost understood that to be relieved of the beast it would be necessary to kill it. The ghost just didn't have the heart for that.

That's when the rationalizations began. The ghost thought he might train and tame the lizard. He thought perhaps he could release it gradually. The angel insisted the gradual approach would not work, as this little red lizard was a very good liar. It was either the death of the lizard or the defeat of the ghost.

Finally, the ghost gave the angel permission to remove the lizard. The lizard screamed as it was twisted from the shoulder it clung to. With one great twist of the wrist, the angel sent it directly to the ground, where the impact broke its back. Then an amazing thing happened. The ghost suddenly became a perfect

"a very good liar"

man and the limp, dead lizard was transformed into a very-much-alive silver and gold stallion. The new man leaped onto the great horse, and they rode off into the distance.

As the Teacher in Lewis's book explains, "What is a lizard compared with a stallion? Lust is a weak, poor, whimpering whispering thing compared with that richness and energy of desire which will arise when lust has been killed."

Up until the age of fifteen, I never doubted God's ability to lead me and use me. During the course of my relationship with Michael, that confidence was shattered into a million pieces. I was not able to pick up those pieces because a little lizard on my shoulder was whispering the most horrible things into my ears. "You cannot break up with him. Don't be a hypocrite. Come on. You won't do that again. What will you tell your friends about why you broke up? Oh, you might want to stop teaching Sunday school until you get this little thing worked out and, by all means, don't even think of teaching Christian clubs. It's not that you're really bad, but what kind of an example would it be if you were found out? You need to save those jobs for the truly pure in heart."

I want you to know what I did not know when I was trapped in my sin. I acted so much like Adam and Eve did when they took that forbidden fruit. I hid. I felt as if God had no use for me now that I had fallen. Yes, there were consequences. But just as God walked through the garden lovingly looking for His dear Adam and Eve, He was eager to bring me back into a loving relationship with Him. He was like that angel, just waiting to break the neck of that little, lying lizard, lust. I was just not having much luck getting the nerve up to give Him permission.

Write Your Story

What about you? What's the name of the little lizard in your life? Lust? Outright sex? Heavy petting? Boy craziness? Language? Bingeing and purging? Anger? Materialism? Stop right now and visualize that little slimy lizard on your shoulder. Then look directly into the eyes of God, who can free you from it and just say, "I'm helpless here. What comes next?"

it's your
turn

Go ahead. Grab your journal and write about it. Please do it.

CHAPTER FIVE

BREAKIN'
UP IS
HARD
TO DO

breaking off

sinful

relationships

in three

steps

BREAKIN' UP
IS HARD
TO DO

Breaking Off Sinful Relationships in Three Steps

*Throw off your old evil nature and your former way of
life, which is rotten through and through, full of lust
and deception. Instead, there must be a spiritual
renewal of your thoughts and attitudes. You must
display a new nature because you are a new person,
created in God's likeness—righteous, holy and true.*

(EPHESIANS 4:22-24 NLT)

"*Just look at this,*" I said, irritated with my lack of
self-control. "My journal is full of it. Break up . . . make up
. . . break up . . . make up."

I handed my journal to Lisa Payne, pointing to the most
recent set of entries.

1-23 ... *It's over. Michael and I told each other we loved each other
several times. And I know we do. I know this is right, but it
doesn't take the hurt away.*

1-24 ... *We are together again. Crazy, huh? He called at midnight last
night and we "worked it out."*

1-26 ... *My spiritual condition has only worsened. I want to be in God's
will, but I'm only half way there so I'm not at all there.*

Lisa closed the journal and gave me a penetrating glance. In that split second we both remembered that breakup that had happened ten months previously. We had spent that night sitting together crying and holding each other.

She had recently lost her father to cancer. I felt like I'd lost my heart to a spiritual cancer. In our individual pain, we had felt the other person's pain. I remembered telling her how stupid I felt crying over a stupid boyfriend when her pain was caused by a much more significant loss.

"Hey, at least I have someone to bawl with," she had sniffled, passing me a new box of tissues. We both laughed that really great, freeing laugh that only comes to visit in the midst of a good, long cry.

Then hours later he had called. We'd gotten back together and I felt really rotten for leaving her alone in her moment of pain, while I waltzed back down the easy road.

"Well," she said, snapping me back to the present. "You know what you have to do. Break this relationship off for good. I'm not going to make this easy for you this time."

Lisa was always saying, "Personhood before partnership!" It was her dating motto, and a good one at that. My relationship was clearly one that put partnership before my own personal development and, unfortunately, my relationship with God.

"You're a great friend," I said sarcastically. I reached for the telephone. It seemed as if it took an hour for my heavy hand to reach the receiver. I dialed his number, then looked at Lisa. She was standing at the door ready to leave, offering me a few moments alone to do what needed to be done.

"Hello," said the warm, familiar voice that I felt belonged to me.

"Hi," was all I could get out.

"What's wrong?" he said, reading my voice without hesitation.

I was silent.

"Dannah," he said, pleadingly.

How I love to hear him say my name, I thought. *Maybe I can talk to him for a few minutes first . . . absorb the last few moments of an "us."*

"Dannah!" he pushed.

"It's over," I said coldly, like a child releasing an animal back into the wild, knowing only a cruel release would send him off. "I do not want this anymore. Our relationship is not what God wants for our lives right now," I said. "You have got to let go too."

He was silent. He'd never been silent before. I believed that his desire was also to live within God's blessing, and he understood that meant ending our relationship.

After a few moments, we both quietly hung up the telephone. I reached for my journal to cry out to my God as tears fell silently down my cheeks.

11-20...*My heart is cold and numb. I mean it's so intense I feel an actual heaviness in my chest. Lord, in Your heavenly plan, what are You teaching me? How long does it take? My will crosses Yours. My will has to die.*

Lisa had come back. She wrapped her arms around me, and I collapsed into them. We cried again. This time, he didn't call back.

If you have given your heart or your body to someone, and you have been feeling a twinge of discomfort as you've read the past few chapters, that is probably the Holy Spirit speaking to you. As I write this, I have been asking Him daily to work in *your* life! Is He? Well, you can be 100 percent sure that if He is, it is because He has an awesome plan for your life. It is even greater than what you could possibly imagine. I know you think this guy is the love of your life. You cannot see down the road yet. You cannot see anyone even coming close to this young man, but God has a plan that is soooo much better.

Right now, you have a tough decision to make. It doesn't matter if you've dated for one month or five years or if the relationship became sexual or it was just squeezin' in on your love life with Jesus, breakin' up is hard to do!

But Scripture is clear over and over again that we *must* walk away from anything that hinders our love for God. The verse above says to "throw" off your former way of life. I know that is not easy. I really cannot make the process less painful for you, but I can give you a step-by-step plan for walking through it.

 ## Tell God

Right before I broke up with my boyfriend, I had gotten into the Word of God. God gave me the strength and conviction to make right choices. He was so tender about it too.

The book of Ezekiel paints a very ugly picture of how hard-hearted Israel had been toward the God who loved them and who considered Himself Israel's Lover. At one point, God told Ezekiel to describe Israel as a helpless, bloodied newborn left lying in a field with the umbilical cord still hanging from it when God showed up to lovingly clean it, clothe it, and care for it. (Kind of gross,

*God can
reach the pain*

I know that
breakin' up is
hard to do.
I know the
pain is
something no
one else can
seem to reach.
Understand
that God can.
"Bare heights
of loneliness
...a wilderness
whose burning
winds sweep
over glowing
sands. What
are they to
Him? Even
there He can
refresh us.
Even there
He can
renew us."

AMY CARMICHAEL
WINDOWS

huh? But God really wanted us to see in that picture that He would love us no matter how he found us.) Then as Israel grew to become a woman, she took God for a brief moment as her Love.

Then she proceeded to take the wonderful garments, jewels, and gifts her Love had made her and give them to her other lovers. This caused great hurt to the God of the universe as again and again Israel chose to love everything but Him. In Ezekiel 11 this great, patient Lover said, "It's time to come back to Me." But how would Israel ever accomplish that? She had had children with her other lovers. She had memories, houses, possessions as a result of her other relationships.

Israel's True Love showed up with a great gift in Ezekiel 11:19 when He said, "I will give them an *undivided* heart." Verse 20 goes on to say, "*Then,* they will . . . be careful to keep my laws. They will be my people, and I will be their God" (italics added).

He knows you have memories. He knows you have possessions, songs, and nicknames. He understands how terribly painful breaking up can be, and He wants to hold your heart in His hands and cause it to be *undivided* so you can go through with it. He does not expect you to prove yourself back into His heart by doing this tough thing without Him and *then* coming into His presence. *Start* by talking to God and receiving His gift of an undivided heart.

What exactly do I mean by an undivided heart? Of course, I am speaking of your heart figuratively, as we often do when we talk of love and devotion. The figurative heart is the central "organ" of your emotional and spiritual life. Let's compare it to the physical heart, which is the central organ of your physical life. When someone's heart is healthy, the four chambers beat in rhythm. What would happen if half of the heart decided it wasn't feeling much like working with the other half? You might have palpitations, or your heart might skip a beat. It could hurt a lot, or you could barely notice it. It would not be an immediate death sentence, but your body would become weaker and weaker if that half of the heart kept resisting the responsibility to do its job in conjunction with the other half. Eventually, that "divided heart" would ruin the quality of your life, and it might one day actually kill you.

Our figurative hearts are like that. I hope that, like me, there was one day when you sat before the great, loving God of the universe and said, "OK, I'm not perfect. I sin. That makes me unworthy of being in Your presence. I know I really deserve death, but thank You so, so much for sending Your dear Son, Jesus, to die in my place. I accept the precious gift of eternal life through His death. From now until eternity, my heart belongs to You!" From that moment on, your figurative heart's job is to pump in tune with the heart of God. But if the side of your heart that handles the emotions gets caught up in an ungodly or distracting relationship, pattern, or habit, you've got the same condition as you would if your physical heart were beating out of sync. Your emotions, spiritual drive, and the quality of life suddenly begin to ebb away. Your figurative heart simply cannot stand to beat out of rhythm any more than your physical heart can.

Write Your Story

Take a moment and beg God for an undivided heart. Even if you don't have a relationship right this very moment but you are consumed with a desire to be with a guy, you must begin to ask for this undivided heart. Go to God. Tell Him about the memories, the hopes, the dreams. Ask Him for an undivided heart.

it's your
turn

Tell a Friend

Just because God begins to work in you does not mean your human heart won't find it very difficult to stay on course. I couldn't have broken up with my boyfriend without Lisa to bear the load with me. She was a very important element in regaining my strength to live a lifestyle of purity.

I suggest you find one or more friends to shoulder the burden for two reasons. They can test what you are thinking and they can enCOURAGE you—or give you courage—to stay on course. You need to talk to that friend *before* you call your boyfriend and give him the chance to pull on your heartstrings.

I still do this in my life. Mostly, I go to my husband and say, "This is what I feel God telling me about this. Can you encourage me?" I also use other wise counselors such as my mother and older godly women to borrow courage. This past week, a special senior higher in my youth group broke up with her boyfriend. She needed to do it, but it was very painful. So she told a Christian friend. The friend encouraged her and suggested she write a letter so she could have everything thought out and so that she could not be sweet-talked out of her commitment. Then the friend told her to make a copy of the letter to go back to for courage in the weeks to come. It was good advice from a good friend.

Tell a friend what you sense God saying so that you can test it and so that the friend will enCOURAGE you to go through with it.

Make a Fast, Strategic Exit

I wish we could ask Joseph about Potiphar's wife. She was one of the richest and most popular women in Egypt. I bet she took Egyptian mud baths and had her feet waxed to keep off the dust. Come to think of it, she probably never walked through the dust. They probably carried her around Egypt in some kind of gold-plated seat. I envision milky skin and jet black hair in that classic Egyptian cut. In fact, she may have started that hairstyle craze. Do you get where I'm going? I think she was a hot item! But in Genesis 39, Joseph didn't think twice about running . . . and fast.

If you have a relationship that provides you with the temptation to sin or that simply distracts you from your love for God, it needs to be discontinued immediately. Joseph is a great example of a man who knew how to make a fast, strategic exit.

I am very proud of a girl named Lana. She was a brand-new, baby Christian when she came to my retreat. Her current boyfriend had introduced her to Jesus. At the retreat, she admitted that there was pressure in the relationship to be physical despite the fact that they both loved God so much. The day after the retreat she broke up with him. Now that's a fast, strategic exit that would have impressed Joseph. Guess what? Shortly after the retreat her "ex" got a girl pregnant. He had to quit college to get a job. That could have been Lana, but it wasn't. Frighteningly, Lana is one of many girls who attended my retreat with that exact story.

Where do you stand with this issue of breakin' up? Is there a relationship you have had in the recent past that still causes pain? Go to God for an undivided heart and find a friend to give you courage. Are you still in a relationship that needs to be ended? Start with an intense talk with God and beg for that undivided heart, then find a friend to borrow courage and make

that fast, strategic exit. Maybe you are not in or have never been in a relationship that needs cut off. Bravo! The seven secrets are just around the corner, and they can help you never have to make this choice.

"Repent, then, and turn to God, so that your sins may be wiped out, that times of refreshing may come from the Lord" (ACTS 3:19).

secret 1

PURITY
IS A
PROCESS

defining

innocence

and

purity

1

secret

PURITY
IS A
PROCESS

Defining Innocence and Purity

God desires "that you may
become blameless and pure"
(PHILIPPIANS 2:15, BOLD ADDED)

 *"Hey, Dannah!" called Jim, a blond, muscular college* student I'd recently met. I walked over to meet him. He said, "John, Dan, and I are gonna grill some steaks for dinner right now. You game? It's on me."

If he was asking me out, I wasn't ready. If he was just being nice, I didn't want to impose. I had stayed in Cedarville for a few weeks of the summer to finish the yearbook. In this tiny town, it was common courtesy for summer students to hang together since there wasn't much to do.

I juggled the stack of files I was carrying to my left hip as I fumbled for my keys . . . and for a response.

"Well, actually I just ordered a pizza for myself. I should probably be here when it arrives, don't you think?" I laughed.

Cool response, Dannah, I thought. *Didn't reflect your discomfort at all. Good line.* And it was true. The pizza was on its way.

"Maybe next time," said Jim with a wave as he walked away.

The truth was, I wasn't so sure about getting back into the dating arena. For now that meant avoiding guys altogether since I knew my tendency was to cling to one if I had the chance. I had really blown it before, and I was having a lot of fun being single. I was going to have a game plan next time. I wasn't ready quite yet.

Down in the yearbook office, I pulled my journal and my Bible out of my sack. My yearbook office had proven to be a quiet respite with God over and over again. I read through some of the entries of the past year.

> 9-15 ... *I yearn for someone to hold me . . . to make it better. I want to back up and change time and make everything perfect. Why me, Lord? Why have You chosen me to know the things I have known? Can I make a difference? There is a thick layer of dusty secrets on my heart. Only You can know them. Only You can reach within and wash it away . . . only You.*

I reached for my pen and my Bible. I felt quite different now. I was sitting before the great God of the universe, and He was teaching me to say no to worldly passions and to live a lifestyle of purity. I began to write:

> *I am pure! The Lord has completely purified me. I John 2:28; 3:1–3: "Now, dear children, continue in him . . . confident and unashamed. . . . How great is the love the Father has lavished on us. . . .When [Christ] appears, we shall be like him. . . . Everyone who has this hope in him purifies himself, just as he is pure."*

May I ask you something? Do you ever feel as if you've totally missed the mark? Like you've messed up the perfection that God started with when you were born? Like you have contaminated the goodness He created in you? Maybe it is something small and silly that makes you feel inferior. Maybe it's a huge secret, a sexual sin that keeps you cowering in your walk with God. Memories can be more convicting than any judge or jury.

I went through a real period of struggling with my own purity at the beginning of my college years. I thought I had completely blown it. Memories came back to haunt me and make me feel inferior. In my mind, I was no longer pure. I had ruined the perfection God had created in me. Let's test that against Scripture for a second . . .

"Surely I was sinful at birth, sinful from the time my mother conceived me" (Psalm 51:5).

"All have sinned and fall short of the glory of God" (Romans 3:23).

"There is not a righteous man on earth who does what is right and never sins" (Ecclesiastes 7:20).

OK, you weren't born yesterday, so you can handle this . . . *you weren't born pure.* You were innocent when you were born, but Scripture says you were born sinful. So this notion that you have "lost" your purity is nonsense. You never had it.

I love the way Kaye Briscoe King, an author and a Christian counselor, looks at this whole issue.[1] She has developed The Journey Spiral (see illustration) upon which she says we "travel" our life's journey, hopefully ending in the dead center of the spiral where we have become truly Christlike. (Stick with me on this. It gets a little deep, but this knowledge is really freeing.)

See that line wiggling across the bottom of the graphic? That represents you or me before we knew Christ

Adapted from "Journey: Wolfing into Wholeness: Body, Mind and Spirit" by Kaye Briscoe King. It has been modified and simplified for this book.

Jesus as our loving Lord and Savior. The moment we commit our lives to Christ and accept His precious blood as payment for our own sad, sinful nature, we begin the exciting journey toward becoming Christlike. That's the first step toward becoming pure, since Christ was pure in every way. I feel very strongly that without Jesus it is not possible to live a lifestyle of purity. I know young women who have some yucky stuff in their past but whose lifestyles exude purity. And I know young women who think they are pure in a very technical sense but whose lifestyles are anything but pure. Innocence is where you begin, and it is possible that you have lost some of your innocence, but purity . . . that's where you end up!

The characters that cross the spiral represent the sins we repeatedly struggle with. Let's name just one—Lust. Each of us was born with Lust hanging around. The dude was sitting there waiting for us to get to him. When we choose to journey toward a close relationship with God (and more often when we do not), he rears his ugly head.

One of three things will happen when you meet Lust. You'll breeze past him with God's help. Or he'll taunt and tease you pretty effectively, maybe causing you to sin, but you eventually struggle past him. Or you get stuck there with him for a long, long, long time.

Hopefully you make it past him and say, "Whew! Made it." And you journey on. But suddenly one day, you notice (because you are walking in a spiral) that there he is again. He doesn't look quite as scary because you have seen him before and God helped you win the battle with him then. So you tell him, *No way! I fought with you before. You're a part of the past.* But there he is and you have to go on.

This happened to me Monday night. At 11:00 at night, I let myself get fooled into thinking that I needed to watch *Beverly Hills 90210,* thinking it was "research" for this book. That television show got me feeling desires, thinking thoughts, dreaming dreams . . . none of which were A-OK. Since my husband was on a trip, I crawled into bed alone, and I thought, *I am either going to fantasize myself to sleep or I am going to tell Lust no!* I mumbled, "God, I'm too sleepy to fight this off. Help me, please! I have seen this monster before, and he doesn't look so big and scary anymore, but I could easily play his game tonight." I reached for the nearest book, forcing my mind to read rather than think, and I soon fell asleep. The next day, I admitted it to my mom and felt really great for not giving in to Lust. (See that pattern? Tell God, Tell a Friend, Make a Fast Strategic Exit—which for me was reading some boring poetry.)

The good news is that each and every evil dude we face on our journey can (like C. S. Lewis's little red lizard) be completely transformed. As you make right choices and follow the pattern to tell God, tell a friend, and make a fast, strategic exit, that wimpy little beast turns into something wonderful for God. It becomes the character that God originally created to dwell within you but that was marred and manipulated when sin entered into the world . . . and into you and me. As you confront lust and make right choices with the help of God and friends and lots of fast, strategic exits . . . that little monster, Lust, slowly becomes God's originally created, contented, uncompromised companion—Purity.

I felt so relieved when I first had the Spiral explained to me. You see, I felt guilty for always running into Lust. He was smaller and his roar less threatening each time, but he kept showing up. The fact that he showed up to taunt me, I learned, was not my sin—it was a given and a chance to walk deeper into the spiral and closer to my dear God *if* I said "no" to lust. Purity is a process.

What a freeing secret . . .

- I was not born pure.

- I will face the beast of Lust, perhaps over and over again, but that in itself is not a sin. Rather it is a chance to develop my purity by talking to God, talking to a friend, and making a fast, strategic exit.

- I can *become* pure.

I think it is extremely important that you grasp this. Understand that you are going to run into this guy Lust someday. Be ready for him and know that saying no to him is what pushes you in that direction toward purity.

Understanding that purity is a process is the first secret toward living a lifestyle of purity, but it is just head knowledge. You need practical how-to skills to get you there. So keep reading. The next secret is not only very practical, but also a great deal of fun.

NOTE
1. Kaye Briscoe King, *Journey: Wolfing into Wholeness: Body, Mind and Spirit* (Dallas: Kaye Briscoe King, 1994), 67–68.

secret 2

PURITY
DREAMS
OF ITS
FUTURE

envisioning

a godly

husband

secret 2

PURITY DREAMS
OF ITS FUTURE

Envisioning a Godly Husband

In ten minutes, Chad, a very handsome college junior,
would be picking *me* up. Already he had treasured me that
night, as if I was a real princess. He took time to give me all
the details of his careful plans. He found out that I really like
Chinese food and was planning to take me to a very special
Chinese restaurant.

Before I knew it, we were discussing his volunteer work as a
counselor at a crisis pregnancy center while we sipped green tea.

"All of the girls are a little shaken when they first come in," he said. "But
we test them to verify if they are, in fact, pregnant. Missing a menstrual cycle
does not necessarily mean they are pregnant. I am always relieved when I can
tell them it is negative."

Wow! I thought. *Did he just say "menstrual cycle"? This guy is confident and
sensitive. He's not afraid. I like that.* As I ate my chicken and peanuts, he told me
more about what he felt was his calling in the field of psychology.

"You are so sure of what you want to be," I said, amazed at his clear vision.
"I'm still struggling with whether or not I like my major."

"Give it time, Dannah," he encouraged me. "You've got almost three years
to go. I'm nearly finished. I am supposed to know by now."

After dinner, we went to a nearby college campus to watch a movie being
shown on the campus lawn. We sat under the stars on a blanket relaxing together

among hundreds of other college students. There wasn't any pressure to be near each other. He made me feel comfortable.

"I have something very special planned for dessert," he said as he wrapped the blanket under his arm. He had a really neat way of making everything seem special. Well, no, he had a really neat way of making *me* feel special.

He drove me to a bakery where he knew the ladies who were baking. I could tell that he came often and that they loved him. After carefully selecting our pastries, he took me to his apartment, where he introduced me to his roommates and then banished them to their rooms while he made homemade hot cocoa for us. We ended the night sipping the cocoa, which was accompanied by equally delicious conversation.

The next day, he wrote *me* a thank-you note for the wonderful evening.

Though it was one of the greatest dates of my life, the next day I had come to a sure conclusion.

I heard my mother's voice as if she were standing next to me, "Dannah, dating is not a game. It's not about casually playing with someone's heart. If you don't intend to marry him, don't date him. Know what you are looking for and only date the guy that fits that dream."

The day she had told me that, I'd written what I called a "shopping list for HIM." My words on this rugged piece of rose-colored stationery drew a picture of the man of my dreams. Chad was a perfect fit spiritually, meeting my dream of a man with a deep commitment to God who deeply desired to serve Him with whatever career he chose. He was obviously physically fit and handsome. (I remembered giggling with Mom when we wrote "Must have cute buns" on my shopping list. We'd left it on the list because it was a memory of our conversation and because physical fitness was important to me.)

But Chad fell short in the personality category. Oh, he had a *great* personality, but he was too much like me. I believed I needed someone who could make me laugh since I was always more prone to "being productive" and "getting my work done."

Chad was a productive guy and would one day have a successful career. I was certain of that. That was his one and only "flaw."

I politely turned down his offer for a second date the following Saturday. I spent the night in my dorm room with a cup of instant hot chocolate thinking how lucky the girl who married Chad would be.

———————⋄•⋄•———————

We live in a world of instant gratification. Want a snack? Pop the microwave open. Want to write a note to a friend? Pop up your e-mail screen. Want a tan? Pop into a tanning bed.

It has been said that one of the main reasons teens today are having sex is because they "can't visualize the future." Can you visualize your future? When you close your eyes do you see the man you will marry?

If you aim for nothing, you'll hit it. Is that how you want to aim for your husband—with an open, blank slate? Or do you want to dream of someone who is just right for you, who complements your weaknesses, and who fulfills your hopes and desires?

That was my choice.

And from the moment I wrote my "shopping list for HIM," I never dated a guy for a second time unless he met the criteria on that list. Each one got *one* chance for me to measure him against the list.

I liked it that way. It took away a lot of the guesswork as far as when to say yes and when to say no, and it didn't give me a chance to hurt him or him a chance to hurt me.

What about you? Do you have a dream? Is he tall, dark, and handsome or blond, rugged, and woodsy? Does he have a lot of drive to be business-minded, or is he a nine-to-fiver who can't wait to clock out to come home to be with you?

It's time to build a vision of your husband-to-be and a vision for how you will honor him on your dates—all of them, not just the ones with him.

Write Your Story
The List: Your Dream

This is one of the really fun parts of this book. Grab a bowl of popcorn, your favorite beverage, a pen, and your journal. You can even grab a friend to do this with you. It can be a lot of fun.

Now, close your eyes and dream.

it's your
turn

His List

Is your character what it ought to be? Are you letting your true personality shine through when you are around guys, or are you putting on a show? Have you taken the time to build some goals and vision for your future? Above all, would he know just by being around you that your faith is strong? How would you measure up if the man who is waiting for you were dreaming of you right now? (He might be, ya know!)

That Physique!

What does he look like? Write it down. Does he work out? Does that matter at all, or not? Does he have short or long hair? Is he unconcerned with his appearance? Is he natural and carefree? Do you see his attractiveness better through his heart than through his physical appearance?

Have fun with this section. Don't hold anything back. But remember to take it lightly. Be willing to be flexible with what you think he should look like. Write it down. Dream, my friend, dream!

Personality Plus!

What is his personality like? If you are not sure, look at your relationship with your girlfriends. Which ones work best and have turned out to be long lasting? Be careful here and get some advice from friends and family. I really let my mom help me here. She pointed out that my best friends were outgoing, humorous, and energetic even though I am more quiet, reserved, and steady. So my husband probably needed to be more crazy and humorous to balance my personality. (And he certainly is!)

It is vital at this point to think through some character qualities that you would require such as "honest" and "committed" and "hardworking." Though they may seem like givens, you will run into guys who don't have what you might expect everyone should have in the character department. I include character issues under "Personality Plus" because it seems to me that personality is often influenced or at least controlled by character or the lack of it.

One thing to consider when you start using

your list is that the outer personality can sometimes hide the true character of a guy. On my "shopping list for HIM," I wrote, "Honest and full of integrity to the point that he even shares with me the bad things. I will love him more if I know what they are and where I stand." My husband's character is deep. He wants to be vulnerably honest. He is easily hurt when someone lies to him or when so-called "friends" desert him. He simply expects that everyone is honest and full of integrity. This part of his character sometimes causes his usual, frisky, puppy-like personality to become quiet and pensive. I did not see that until many, many months into our relationship. He is proof that the most difficult category to "measure" may be "Personality Plus" if you are looking for character.

Dream, my friend. Dream. Write.

His Dreams!

What does he dream of becoming . . . of doing with his life? Is it compatible with your dreams for yourself? (It would not work very well to fall in love with someone who wants to be a lumberjack and live on a mountain with ten kids, if you dream of a high-rise apartment and one child who plays in your office suite.)

Dream.

His Other Love

I hope you will choose not to marry and not to even date someone who is not a Christian or who is not totally living for God. My list, written in November of 1986, is faded and tattered. But I still treasure it and take it to retreats I do for girls so they can read every word. Under this category of His Other Love my list says three things:

1. Being a Christian isn't enough. He must have insight. He must be growing and willing to try to grow.

2. Spiritual leader—He has to be one who will lead me and others. He must lead me in that he prays first and he encourages devotions for us. He must lead others in that he is involved in service (Sunday school, ministering to friends, being an example, etc.).

3. Similar viewpoints—He must take stands like I do for what I do. He must have the same sort of background. (I think I would like it if he was saved early—like me!)

Isn't a relationship with a non-Christian guy a great chance to witness to him?

Yes, it is.
One of my best friends from high school, Bethany Langham, was a hot item in our dating years. She was smart and outgoing, she had the most beautiful skin and the perkiest nose, and her eyes sparkled when she talked. She drove the guys bananas! I once casually introduced her to a friend of mine named Doug who was not a Christian. Doug desperately wanted to date her and aggressively pursued her. Doug was handsome, fun, and equally pursued by a great number of girls, but Bethany's line had been

(continued on page 69)

For me, it was a given that he was going to be a Christian. I wanted to define that a little more with some specific things. I often wrote of this in my journal.

11-25-87 . . .
I have no doubt . . . the only reason for marriage is because two can serve God more effectively together than apart. A frightening standard . . . one I can see deceiving myself out of. Few find this relationship. Few need it.

It was so important to me that my husband be a man who was really "going for God." I hope that you want that too. It will save you a lot of heartache in years to come.

Let me tell you why the standard of dating someone who says he is a "Christian" is not enough. I know a woman named Mary. Everywhere I went for years I heard about her. Then I finally met her when she spoke at an event I attended. I could see right away why she was always brought up in conversation. She was blonde, beautiful, and oozed with a contagious enthusiasm. Her speaking style made me envious because she had the skill to make us laugh and cry as she wanted. She talked a lot about her marriage. In college, her husband was a handsome, popular student who had it bad for her. He told her he was a Christian, but she couldn't see a whole lot of "fruit" to back it up. Still, he intrigued and attracted her. Eventually they got married.

Today, he easily confesses that he told her he was a Christian to get her to date him and mostly to get her to sleep with him. Their marriage is filled with pain as he rejects God, desires more to fulfill his own selfish wishes than to love and nurture her, and even suggested they abort their fourth child because it was an inconvenience to him. Though she has a vibrant testimony and is a great encouragement to many, she wishes desperately she had listened to "the little voice inside" of her (probably the Holy Spirit) that told her he "was just saying" he was a Christian.

Be safe. Set a high, high standard in this area. I know that some of you are not doing so. According to a national survey of religiously active girls, some of you have no problem dating someone of "another religion."[1]

What does God say? Second Corinthians 6:14 says, "Do not be yoked together with unbelievers." That makes it clear that it's not a good idea to date someone who does not know God and His Son, since dating really is the first step toward marriage. You should not step in that direction with anyone unless he shares your faith. You run the risk of falling in love with someone you simply cannot have. Let me ask you something: Do you want to be intellectually and spiritually superior to the man you fall in love with, *or* do you want to be challenged and stimulated by him forever and ever? That is entirely your choice.

I am happy to say that eventually, God did bring a man into my life who was everything I dreamed of in that list. It was really neat to write, "You are everything" across the list and present it to him one day.

One day you will probably find the spe-

(from page 68)

drawn. Each night that he called to again beg her for a date, she was blunt about it, "Doug, I think you're a great guy, but I need to tell you that I cannot date someone who does not believe what I believe about God." This turned into long inquiries from him about God. Bethany still believes those were his ploys to get her to stay on the phone with him, but she took it as a chance to read him Scripture, pray over him, and blow his mind with the truth of God.

But Bethany never, never dated Doug . . . not once. She had her vision for the man she would marry, and it included a godly leader who would challenge, stimulate, and protect her spiritually for the rest of her life. And she got it when she found Jeff Whitcomb, a great big strapping, godly man who all but worships her. I wonder if she would have gotten what she wanted if she hadn't stuck to her dream in every dating opportunity.

cial one that God has created just for you. Until then, pray for him.

I read in the July 1999 issue of *Focus on the Family* about Dolores Cummins of Lindale, Texas, who prayed for her husband before she ever met him. She wrote, "The air was cold that December night. Church bells reminded us to pray for boys trapped in the Battle of the Bulge. I was 15, but I remember hearing a voice saying, 'Your future husband is in that battle—pray!' A year later, I met my Robert. We started dating, and later we married. To my amazement, he related his experience of lying facedown in a beet field during that battle. The Germans bayoneted nearly all of his fellow soldiers, but they simply stepped over him, sparing his life." I have no doubt that God used her prayers to protect him.

Take a moment right now to start the habit of praying for your future husband. Pray that God would protect him in the physical battles that he faces, but especially the spiritual battles. Pray that God would protect his mind, his body, and his soul until the day that you find him.

Go ahead. Take a moment right now to pray for him.

If the story God writes with your love life is anything like mine, finding him (or waiting for God to bring him to you) will be hard, but not nearly as hard as what follows. It was after I found my husband-to-be that the rest of the secrets became so difficult to execute. But they are worth knowing, because not only did they keep me living a lifestyle of purity, but they also kept him really desiring to pursue me.

NOTE
1. Eugene C. Roehlkepartain, ed. *The Youth Ministry Resource Book* (Loveland, Colo. : Group, 1988), 44.

secret 3

PURITY IS
GOVERNED
BY ITS
VALUE

CHAPTER EIGHT

part a:

discovering

your value

in God's

eyes

secret 3

PURITY IS
GOVERNED BY
ITS VALUE

Part A: Discovering Your Value in God's Eyes

> *The king is enthralled by your beauty; honor him,*
> *for he is your lord. . . . All glorious is the princess*
> *within her chamber; her gown is interwoven with gold.*
> *In embroidered garments she is led to the king.*
> (PSALM 45:11, 13-14)

The pile of textbooks and syllabi on my desk looked like Mt. Everest, so I'd made the choice to be a responsible college student on this Saturday evening. That was three hours ago, and I'd decided I didn't realize how long Saturday night could get. I sat alone in a massive dorm that was normally full of a couple hundred chattering college girls. Trying to concentrate on my Organizational Communication paper only made the silence more deafening. I needed a friend.

I tried Kimberly. Her roommate answered. "Sorry, Dannah," she said, seeming to know how I felt. "She's out with Jake tonight. I think she took a late pass, so she probably won't be back until after midnight."

I dialed Troy VanLiere's dorm, sure I was going to get some nutty Bethel guy other than him.

Why does he live in that place anyway? I wondered.

I let it ring a long time. No answer.

My fingers ran through the college phone book. Someone I knew had to be around. I stopped at the *G*s.

"Bob Gresh!" I exclaimed. "He'll be around."

It was the running joke that he and his gang could never make up their minds quite what to do. They spent so much time talking about it, they almost never got around to doing anything before it was too late.

I dialed Bob's number in hopes that it was his room they'd decided to deliberate in tonight.

"Hey, what's shakin'?" answered the crazy, familiar voice.

"Hi, Bob! It's me, Dannah," I said. "I'm dateless, friendless, and bored. I need a friend to talk to, and friends are a little scarce around here on a Saturday night."

I'd met Bob nine months previously in Mrs. Harner's Advanced Composition class. He was a comfortable friend. I liked him because he was the class clown, but being in his writing group allowed me a peek into his serious nature. He wasn't just funny and outgoing. His writing told me that he was full of character and conviction. He had vision and was driven to see it through. He was emotional and tenderhearted. He had an uncompromised passion for God. I really respected him.

"When are you going to admit that you are going to marry me?" he asked.

"You are always saying that, silly," I laughed. He was, too, but neither of us thought it meant anything. He was always saying something that meant nothing to get a good laugh.

"I'll be right over," he said.

"What?" I responded.

"We're going on a date," he informed me.

An hour later we were sitting on a park bench eating the very last of our Crazy Bread and sharing a Frosty. We laughed about Advanced Composition. We showed each other pictures of our families. He acted funny. I laughed at him. We talked about our dreams.

"You're a cheap date," he said, throwing away our trash, as if the conversation was getting a little too deep for him. "I don't mean that in a bad sense, just that you're easily contented."

"This is *not* a date," I said adamantly, smiling at his sudden discomfort at the thought that he may have offended me.

He comfortably reached over and kissed me. It was warm and wonderful, but very unfamiliar.

"*Now* do you think this is a date, Dannah Barker?" he asked as he gazed intently into my eyes.

I wish you were here with me right now. I would pamper you nearly to death. I would grab some of my favorite hand lotion—probably pear- or peach-scented—and I would give you a wonderful hand massage all the way up to your elbows. Then I would take you into my dining room where I would have the table covered in silk and lace. Dainty, valuable teacups would be waiting for us with your favorite steaming tea at the perfect temperature. I would have Godiva biscuits lying in a crystal bowl near your table setting. Close your eyes and go there with me.

Rub your own hands and relax.

Hear the relaxing music in the background.

Imagine the beautiful teacup as you lift it to your lips.

Crunch into that delicious biscuit, smothered in just the right amount of chocolate. Mmmmmm! This is excellent. I feel pampered. Do you?

Oh, wake up! All I really gave you was a lousy bag of dead leaves in some hot water. That's it! (OK, the Godiva was a bit costly.) But it was not what I gave to you that made you feel special. It was *how* I gave it. The lace and silk and fine china cups gave value to the actual gift. How I presented everything was what made you feel valued.

You see, I could have walked down the hall outside my office to a cold steel machine and, after plunking a few coins into it, brought you a Styrofoam cup full of tea leaves and hot water. There would be no great memories there. I gave you something "trashable."

I could have driven you to the local coffee shop and ordered us a ceramic mug of hot tea and maybe a bagel or something to go with it. That would be OK, but if the mug broke or we never got to go there again, no

Styrofoam Cup, Ceramic Mug, or Priceless Teacup?

Take this quick test. Decide in each category whether you are a Styrofoam cup, a ceramic mug, or a priceless teacup. Fill in the box with the appropriate letter. (S=Styrofoam, C=Ceramic, T=Teacup)

☐	In the way I dress
☐	In the movies I watch
☐	In the television shows I watch
☐	In the material I view on the Internet
☐	In the way I talk to girls about guys
☐	In the places I am willing to go on dates
☐	In the things I am willing to do on dates
☐	In the things I talk about on dates
☐	In the length of time it takes me to a give a guy my heart
☐	In the way I treat friends when a dating opportunity pops up
☐	In the way I spend time with God specifically talking to Him about guys

How did you do? Hold that thought. We'll come back to it.

big deal. The mug wasn't treasured and valued in the highest sense.

But pull in the fine china and silk and lace and Godiva treats and we have a memory that we want to keep around. You and I would both be crushed if one of those precious cups broke. They are treasured possessions to us.

Let me ask you something. In your dating relationships, are you a "trashable" Styrofoam cup, an everyday ceramic mug that is easily replaceable, or a valuable, priceless teacup? It's all in the presentation.

I've heard the saying, "Every great love story ends in tragedy" many times lately. Of course, you can quickly point to the very dead Romeo and Juliet as a prime example of this statement. But I'm a hopeless romantic and I don't want to believe that, so I took time to line up some proof that not all great love stories end in tragedy. I found some that don't!

Little Women is really three great love stories that end happily. (Even the story of Jo and Laurie ends happily since they don't do anything they regret.) You can read the classic version by Louisa May Alcott and get the full picture of the great story, or you can rent the video version starring Winona Ryder for a faster but just as heart-stirring look at the characters' love stories.

Sense and Sensibility is the fantastic love story of two sisters and their husbands-to-be that also ends happily. Again, you can read the classic by Jane Austen if you are a good reader, or you can rent the video version starring Emma Thompson. They're both fantastic.

Passion and Purity is a fabulous book detailing the love story of Jim and Elisabeth Elliot. It was also my "handbook" to sexual purity through my college years. Be sure to find a copy of this one.

What I have concluded, as I have read these stories and others, is that great love stories do not have to end in tragedy. However, *a flame of pain fuels every great love story.* The pain comes in one of two packages.

The Crash and Burn

Your first choice is to have a relationship that is an easy road of blissful moments. The problem is that the relationship could potentially end in a fuel fire of pain. These love stories are written by women who are Styrofoam cups and, sometimes, ceramic mugs. Romeo and Juliet are a great example of this. Juliet wears her heart on her sleeve and throws every caution to the wind to be with Romeo. She defies her parents, sneaks around to be with him, and makes easy, heart-defining choices to have secret moments of bliss with Romeo. In the end, they commit suicide because their relationship is opposed. I do like the story, but I sure would not want it to be *my* great love story. Where's the sunset? Where's the happily-ever-after? (Where's their pulse?)

The girls I have met who choose to make easy, heart-defining choices seem to have no sense of self-value. They are trying desperately to get some kind of guy to desire them at about any cost. Unfortunately, these are often the girls who get trashed at the end of the relationship because they didn't convey any sense of self-value to the guy. I hope you will not choose the crash and burn.

The Pure, Slow Burn

You can have the sunset love story in your life, but it will mean that you choose the pain that comes in package number two—the pure, slow burn. The pain here is caused by your own self-control, which really feels much like self-denial. As you guard your heart and your body, you can expect to experience some pain. It is far easier, short-term, to be the girl who throws caution to the wind and lets her heart and body become tangled into the moment. *But* if your great love story is fueled by the pain that is caused by wise, head-defined choices in the beginning, it may come with a blissful, happily-ever-after ending. If the relationship does end? You will have no regrets because you have not given your heart or your body away. (And there are still lots of nice clean pages upon which to keep writing your story. One broken relationship is not the end!)

Sense and Sensibility is a great portrait of this kind of love story, but what is so masterful about this classic is that it is laced also with a tragic love story. Elinor is the older sister who falls madly in love with Edward, who is handsome, wealthy, and good-hearted. Throughout her relationship, she is governed by the strictest of choices. She does not allow her heart to be seen. Unfortunately, prior to meeting her, Edward was secretly engaged to another. Being an honorable man, he knows he must not shame the young woman who no longer owns his heart. (I know that sounds ridiculous, but it was written in a different day and age. Stick with me!) Elinor is careful to allow him to remain honorable by not manipulating his heart but by standing free and proud on her own.

Her sister Marianne, on the other hand, falls for Willoughby and lets everyone know it as they race off in his carriage day after day and as she sends him a ridiculous number of unanswered notes. In a great twist, Willoughby marries another for her wealth and leaves Marianne crying at her loss of love, not to mention her loss of integrity.

Meanwhile Elinor takes a call from Edward, who she thinks is married but who has been honorably freed from his commitment. He comes to ask on bended knee for her hand in marriage. A wedding carriage, fresh flower petals, and white horses escort them into the happily-ever-after.

I love Psalm 45. It was written as a wedding song and was probably sung at many Jewish weddings in the days of King David. It's also a wonderful figurative example of what God sees when He looks at you and me . . . the bride of Christ. He looks upon you and sees a princess. You are a princess. A princess enjoys the great benefits of being waited upon and being adorned with rich tapestry. In my mind, she is calm and contented with where she is today because she knows she is the princess and will someday be married to a marvelous prince.

OK, I know sometimes you may feel more like a frog than a princess, but those are just feelings and they will go away. When I was in high school, I never looked in a mirror. I put my makeup on without looking. (How many silly smudges there must have been!) I felt pretty froglike.

Sometime in my college years, I decided that God had done a pretty good job with me, and it became much easier to be governed by my value because I had begun to feel it. It wasn't just about how I looked, but I had begun to accept how I looked as a part of who and what God valued. It *was* about how I was saturating myself with God's truth. As I began to be filled with His presence, I began to feel the value He placed on me.

The point is this. God says you are a princess. He is *enthralled* by your beauty. Do you believe that? Do you trust the God who made you to be a better judge of your value than the way hormonal days, bad friends, and a crazy schedule can sometimes make you *feel?*

You are a princess. Your behavior and the choices you make must be governed by that value if you are aiming for the sunset ending in your love story. You must present yourself as you would priceless china.

What choices will you make to build a great love story? Will they be choices governed by your heart and your feelings, which can lead to tremendous heartbreak and humiliation? Will you present yourself like "trashable" Styrofoam or an everyday ceramic mug? Or will you make choices governed by your head and the knowledge that you are valued as a princess in God's eyes? Will you be highly valued like a precious piece of china?

Sometimes making choices based on your value may hurt a great deal at first, but they offer you the chance of a great happily-ever-after and will always result in *no regrets.*

Write Your Story

Which are you headed for in your life? The crash and burn? The pure, slow burn? Grab your journal and begin with "Based on my own value evaluation, I am headed for the crash and burn/pure, slow burn. Here is why and/or here is what I need to change . . ."

it's your
turn

secret 3

PURITY IS
GOVERNED
BY ITS
VALUE

part b:

demonstrating

your value

in the eyes

of others

secret 3

PURITY IS
GOVERNED BY
ITS VALUE

Part B: Demonstrating Your Value in the Eyes of Others

 *This chapter is for the brave and daring. It's about* respecting the great weakness God has created in guys. They are made to physically yearn for our bodies. That's not to say that you might not experience some of the same yearning for their bodies, but it is usually far more consuming for men. A University of Chicago sex study said that 54 percent of men thought about sex daily—a number that caused humorist Dave Barry to conclude, "The other 46 percent of the men are lying. Because it's a known scientific fact that all men think about sex a minimum of all the time."[1] (Ha!)

I've seen many studies about this and they vary some, but all agree with one thing. Guys think about sex a lot. One figure that is commonly cited states that most guys think about sex every four minutes. I saw a movie preview that poked fun of that study. A girl mentioned the study to a guy. He first denied it and then admitted that it is probably true. She said, "Well, I've been here twenty minutes." (Obviously she was guessing that she may have been the subject of his "thinking.")

In his best-selling book, *I Kissed Dating Goodbye,* Joshua Harris said that his pastor had once asked his youth group to answer the question "How far have you gone?" They did so using a number scale. After the meeting, Joshua overheard some of the guys bragging about how "high" they had "scored" and with whom in the youth group they had reached a certain number.[2] Yikes!

I am not trying to paint a really ugly picture here, but sometimes young women are terribly naive or they deny the overtly sexual desires that God built into guys. That is not to say that you may not have similar desires or that a girl is never the aggressor. But more often than not, guys are more physically aggressive. Sometimes a girl's actions, clothes, and dating choices are perfectly explosive fuels that may cause a relationship to burst into the flames of a tragic ending. That was not the kind of love story I wanted to write with my life. I hope it is not what you will write with yours.

Since you are a princess, you need to be sure to conduct yourself as one! Here are three areas in which I see girls forgetting to present themselves as valuable, priceless princesses.

The Royal Wardrobe

Belly rings. Miniskirts. Short-skirts. Hip-huggers. The fashion world today screams sex for the poor guys out there who struggle to live a lifestyle of purity. Since clothes don't affect girls and women in the same say, we continue to wear the latest trends. If you are like me, it's a bit hard to get perspective on this since the fashion trends stare us down every single day. So let's grab some perspective by looking at another day and age.

Little Women was written when the fashion was to push a young woman's bustline up to her neckline. In the book, beautiful (and normally modest) Meg March went to Annie Moffat's "coming out" party. The other girls attending convinced her to let them dress her, complete with a corset and low-cut neckline.

"do you want to be merely decorative?"

Meg blushed at herself when she looked in the mirror and determined not to let the way she was dressed affect the person she was, *but it did very much affect her.* Into the evening, her neighbor Laurie found her dancing frivolously at every offer, flirting freely, and drinking. (It wasn't punch, either.) He confronted her much like a brother, sarcastically admitting he didn't like the way she was dressed and telling her, "I don't like fuss and feathers."

Later, Laurie apologized for being so harsh with her, and Meg admitted the way she was dressed had made her behave badly, saying, "Take care my skirt doesn't trip you up; it's the plague of my life and I was a goose to wear it." Laurie encouraged her, "Pin it round your neck, and then it will be useful."

In the movie version of *Little Women* starring Winona Ryder, Meg's mother put it all in perspective that night when Meg admitted her misguided fashion statement. Marmie told Meg, "If you feel your value lies in being merely decorative, I fear you will find yourself one day believing that is *all* you really are."

On your dates and in your everyday life, do you want to be merely decorative, a trait that will someday wear away?

I do not want to tell you what I think you should and should not wear. But might I suggest a litmus test for your wardrobe? When you put an outfit on, ask yourself, "Do I feel sexy?" I'm not talking about feeling good or attractive. I am talking about feeling *seductive.* You know what I mean! If you don't know, then you are probably OK. But if you do know, then you probably have a few things in your wardrobe that need to go. If you feel seductive, you probably are, and that can be very dangerous on a date. It will change the way that you behave and the way your date expects you to behave. Be careful in choosing your royal wardrobe.

The Princess's Kingdom

So, you're dressed and ready to go. Where should you go? A princess should always stay within the confines of her own kingdom where she is safely guarded under the watchful eye of her public.

I have a friend named Mark who, when he was dating, knew his weakness was to be consumed with his physical desire. Even in his early twenties, he wanted his dating relationships to be governed by some strict principles. So, when Hannah caught his eye, he asked her father for the right to "court" her. They spent "dates" sitting on the sofa in her parents' living room under watchful and loving eyes. They kissed for the first time at the altar of the Lord Jesus Christ as they exchanged vows to love each other for the rest of their lives. Wow! Doesn't that sound tough?

As I have conducted purity retreats, the girls tell me two things about *where* they will go on dates. First, they tell me that nothing good ever happens when they are alone with guys. Their conclusion is always this: If you are truly serious about guarding your innocence and living a lifestyle of purity, you won't go to an apartment, a house, or anywhere where you are truly alone . . . ever. So, how serious are you? Are you serious enough to stay public with your relationship?

Some of the most memorable dates I had with the man who is now my husband were in a laundry facility.

1-20-87 . . . . *We did our laundry together tonight!*

10-24-87 . . *A special day with my man. I will remember . . . laughing in the laundry-mat!*

*Joshua Harris on
Style & Modesty*

Dannah: *If everyone reading this book were right here with us right now, what would you tell them about how they dress?*

Joshua: *I have spoken about this in public. It is always a hard message to deliver, because I look around and see how Christian girls are dressed and I think I am going to offend so many of them. They need to look at it this way—there are just a lot of ways that we can take things into our own hands and say, "God, I don't think You know what You are doing. Or I don't think You are doing it fast enough." How you dress is one way of showing that you do not trust God. Shannon, my wife, talks about this a lot. She knows girls face the temptation to pick out the shorter skirt in*

(continued on page 87)

Someplace as crazy as a laundry facility can be a place for romance to bud. (Note that I was not just doing his laundry for him. We were doing our laundry *together.*) Anyway, the fact is that we could be monitored by "our public," but we were in our own little world as the washers and dryers dulled the sound of others around us. If you want to spend time getting to know a guy, pick a place where your public can watch you while you talk.

The second thing that girls who attend my retreat tell me is that nothing good ever happens in a horizontal position. Even if other friends are around and they're lounging on a beanbag together, they agree that lying down is a bad line to cross. Lying down is very symbolic of letting your guard down. Don't do it. Stay vertical!

A princess should stay where her public can see her and she should stay vertical.

The Conduct of the Princess

Now you've probably got an idea of whom you will be with, how you will dress, and where you will or won't go. Now, how will you act?

In my very first love relationship at the age of fifteen, I did what I see far too many of my favorite girls doing . . . I wore my heart on my sleeve and left it there for the taking. I later wrote:

11-7-86 . . .

"Be careful of your thoughts, they may break into actions." . . . "Love will always endure if you keep it pure."

Those are two sayings I've heard in the

past two days that were real meaningful to me. It's so easy to fall into bad situations if you don't build up a very straightforward plan of defense. Believe me. I know.

Wearing your heart on your sleeve and not being cautious with your actions is not a good idea. It sets you up for great hurt and, to be honest, guys are not nearly as likely to desperately yearn for you when you are so easily caught! Guys are competitive and have an insatiable need to get what they think they have to earn.

Jill is a freshman in college who is dating an older guy named Jonathan. She has worn her heart all over her sleeve in this relationship. She has told him (and he has told her) that they will be married someday. They've talked of family, dreams, careers, homes, and everything they possibly can. Because they believe they will end up married, they have had a really hard time keeping the relationship pure. I think they just might make it because I see how much they love the Lord and how very much they love each other. But right now, Jonathan is barely interested in pursuing her and they are taking a "break" from the relationship. He's more interested in his band, his friends, and his future. Why shouldn't he be? He already has her right where he wants her. She is heartbroken and finds it difficult to wake up in the morning.

She is experiencing some of the pain that comes because she made choices characteristic of the "crash and burn" in the area of her conduct. She is as committed to him as if she were married to him and finds herself unsatisfied. In having everything she wanted in the

(from page 86)

the closet because they know that it grabs the guy's attention. But girls have a responsibility to their brothers in Christ to help guard their purity. They have a responsibility to the guy. The way you dress makes a huge difference in how a guy views you and how he guards his heart. You have no idea how difficult it is for a guy to look at you with purity in his heart when you are dressed immodestly. I think a lot of you are naive. You don't understand how a male works . . . Christian or non-Christian. You don't know that we are stimulated by sight. You just see the style, ya know? But you run the risk of really defrauding your Christian brother if you reach for the immodest outfit. If you could just see where girls who dress immodestly lead guys mentally. I have had girls come up to me after I speak about this and say, "I have heard my mom and dad tell me this . . . but hearing it from a guy really changes it for me." Then, later they send letters that said, "I went through [my closet] and I threw away these outfits." That's great!

relationship very quickly, she found herself in a period where she has nothing of the relationship. She forgot that she was single. She forgot that she belongs to herself and God during this "season" of her life.

Joshua Harris said, "God gives us singleness—a season of our lives unmatched in its boundless opportunities for growth, learning, and service—and we view it as a chance to get bogged down in finding and keeping boyfriends and girlfriends. But we don't find real beauty of singleness in pursuing romance with as many different people as we want. We find the real beauty in using our freedom to serve God with abandon."[3]

My friend, carefully analyzing the royal wardrobe and staying in the eyes of the public are the easiest things to govern because they are very definable. Determining to remain single in your mind and your heart until there is a ring on your finger is a much harder element to govern. It requires you to bridle your heart for a time, but I can promise that in the waiting you will find a healthy, growing pain as opposed to the destructive pain of giving your heart away too soon and having it shattered.

Take a look at the women in the Bible. The ones with the big headlines are most often those who bridled their hearts to make wise head choices in relationships. Look at Ruth and . . . let's see, what was her sister-in-law's name? Well, the two of them were stuck with their old mother-in-law with no hopes of finding love again. The mother-in-law gave them the chance to follow their hearts and leave. Ruth stayed, though her sister-in-law ran for it. Ruth knew staying was the right thing to do, but it didn't necessarily feel good. Guess what? In the end, God created a rich, beautiful love between her and Boaz *and* they became the great-grandparents of the great King David. Because Ruth was governed by her value and didn't wear her heart on her sleeve, she played a vital role in the lineage of David (and Jesus). Wow! (I wonder what ever happened to her sister-in-law . . . what's-her-face?) What a great love story—far better than the one she may have written with her life if she had forgotten her value and allowed her life to be governed by her heart.

Write Your Story

OK. Now it's time to work it! I'd like you to do three things with your journal. Take your journal into your clothes closet or sit with it next to your dresser or wardrobe. Look through your clothes and kick out what needs to go . . . now! Don't give that stuff to someone else. Trash it. It's Styrofoam cup stuff. Go ahead. I will still be here when you get back. Do it!

it's your ***turn***

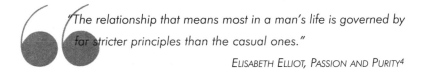

"The relationship that means most in a man's life is governed by far stricter principles than the casual ones."

ELISABETH ELLIOT, *PASSION AND PURITY*[4]

Now, tell God how good that feels. (Or if you didn't have to trash anything, praise Him for keeping you modest whether through your own decision or rules that your parents have.) While you're in there writing, jot down some thoughts on where you can go on a date where you live—places that allow you to stay public!

Finally, talk to God about your heart. Write down the names of people you've given it to and ask God to reclaim it. Trust Him to write a love story beyond your wildest imagination. Determine to be governed by your value, not your heart.

The night that I first "dated" Bob, I knew I needed to be governed by my value. I could tell that he fit my list and I was interested in dating him—for "real," next time. But I had really blown it. *I* had called *him* . . . how desperate does that look? I let him *kiss* me on our first date . . . how easy does that seem? I was determined to begin to make some tough choices that better reflected my value. That might mean fewer blissful moments but had the promise of a happily-ever-after ending loosely attached.

The next time I saw Bob after I realized my poor beginning, I had the List *and* I was ready to let my value in God's eyes govern my behavior. He drove by in his little white sports car, backing up when he saw me. I was walking away from him on the pathway to my dorm.

"Hey, Dannah Barker, come here," he called. My heart jumped and every muscle ached to turn and hop into that car like I had so many times in the past few weeks.

"Why?" I probed.

"Because you adore me," he claimed.

"Oh, do I?" I smiled at him and then turned to keep walking.

"Dannah Barker, come back here," he called as I calmly kept walking toward my destination.

"Chase me!" I challenged and confidently walked into my dorm.

9 Sexual intercourse

8 "Experimental" nakedness

7 Petting while clothed

6 Open-mouthed, passionate kissing. A new desire awakens with this.

5 Kissing on the cheek or softly kissing on the lips. These are sweet, innocent signs of affection.

4 Hands on shoulders and hands on waist. A definite sign that romance is in the air.

3 Holding hands. This is a nice sign of attachment. It says you like each other. Your relationship is growing.

2 Talking with a guy. Remember to "stock up" for really comfortable and fascinating conversation.

1 Looking at a guy and making eye contact. A good sign that they are interested in you is that they smile and look right back at ya babe!

Steps to Physical Intimacy

Be governed by your value. Like a priceless piece of china, the way you present yourself deserves great care. Take the time to carefully draw a firm, uncrossable line, using the suggestions on the next page.

Adapted from Greg Johnson and Susie Shellenberger, *What Hollywood Won't Tell You About Sex, Love and Dating* (Venture: Regal, 1994).

The Line

If you truly are "governed by your value," you should never find yourself in a compromising situation. Unfortunately, I know some of you will find yourselves in that position, anyway. Are you prepared to stop things? Let's walk through this together. Look at the "steps to physical intimacy" sidebar.

1. *Draw a firm black line right above the step where you will stop any type of physical contact.* Predetermining where you will stop things will help you when temptations arise. It will set off a mental alarm for you. (Remember, God designed you and me to naturally desire to move to the next step. It is not easy to stop the desire to progress. Be very conservative–oh, what a word–about where you draw this firm black line!)

2. *Now, take time to prayerfully consider . . . would God be pleased to see you doing the particular physical activity directly below that firm black line?* If you have any doubt at all, go back to number one and reconsider your choice. Remember God desires that you do not have even a "hint" of sexual immorality within your life.

3. *Finally, let me suggest the option of drawing a line at a lower level of physical activity for before you are engaged.* For example, let's say you drew your firm black line above number five. You have determined that your firm black line will remind you to stop as soon as soft kissing begins to turn into something more passionate. I desire for you to unquestionably not go beyond that line when you are engaged. That can be hard. Your body and your mind are tellin' you that you've almost made it and temptation can really blindside you. (But, oh, you *have* almost made it. Don't blow it here.) I am not saying you have to, but wouldn't it be neat to save that special intimacy for your engagement! Push yourself. Draw a dotted line at a lower level and determine not to go beyond that line until you are engaged.

What decisions do you need to make in your current dating behavior that will protect you from going too far, too soon? Keep in mind that you must stop before you have any desire to be more physically intimate with someone. For many, that means holding hands is too far.

NOTES
1. Ed Young, Pure Sex (Sisters, Oreg.: Multnomah, 1997), 81.
2. Joshua Harris, I Kissed Dating Goodbye (Sisters, Oreg.: Multnomah, 1997), 88.
3. Ibid., 40–41.
4. Elisabeth Elliot, Passion and Purity (Grand Rapids: Revell, 1984), 136.

secret 4

PURITY
SPEAKS
BOLDLY

CHAPTER TEN

preparing

your

tongue

for dates

secret 4

PURITY
SPEAKS
BOLDLY

Preparing Your Tongue for Dates

10-4 . . . It pays to do things the hard way, which is the case more often than not when you seek the Lord's will. My relationship with Bob Gresh is more unique and special than it ever has been. There are not any "I love yous," there are no physical displays of affection, and yet our relationship runs more deeply now than when those things were present. It's not easy. There are days I don't share with him and yet I'm so thankful that the Lord has given us the wisdom to patiently wait for His timing.

11-13 . . . I argued with Bob tonight. No, we didn't fight, but we enthusiastically debated our views. I never even knew I had it in me. Debate is somehow stimulating. In fact, if we hadn't been disagreeing, I'd have been laughing.

I laid down my journal, having read the slow progression of several months of a relationship I was treasuring. Our hearts, which for a few weeks were so easily read and unguarded in our passion, had relinquished to an unspoken determination by our heads to progress slowly . . . painfully slowly.

However, there was a sense of an upcoming reward to the pain of waiting. I wasn't afraid in this relationship because I was not entirely vulnerable. I felt no risk of becoming overly physical because that was in no way a part of our relationship. And best of all, there were still some incredible moments ahead of us. I did not realize it, but I was about to experience one of them.

I glanced at the clock and realized it was time to meet Bob at my dorm lobby. He met me, escorted me to his car, and got in. As we drove away, the conversation picked up where we'd left off the last time we'd been together. We had a pace to our conversation. It was aggressive and determined. We had no awkward pauses as we wondered what to say next. We were on a mission to chisel into each other's minds and were using words as our primary tool.

Suddenly, he stopped the car. I noticed the soft January snowflakes for the first time and felt the hush of a fresh snowfall embrace our car. It was as if time had suddenly stopped.

He reached over and tenderly kissed the tip of my nose, barely brushing my lips as he pulled away.

"*This* is as far as I want any physical contact to go between us," he whispered and then drove on. We were silent for the first time in months. I pondered the unspoken words he had *not* used to charge me with a great task.

I heard him.

He was asking me to keep talking.

I did.

The tongue is a powerful tool. James compares it to the rudder of a great ship. With just this little instrument, you can set your course for a direction toward something great or toward the perils of an iceberg.

Though somewhat of an introvert, I found that keeping my lips loose kept my relationship headed toward greatness. I've seen a trend as I counsel young women in their relationships. Author Robert Wolgemuth spoke of it in his book, *She Calls Me Daddy*. He said that young women who have learned the art of conversation are less likely to be caught in compromising physical situations. Why? "First, assuming that boys will nearly always be the aggressors, [you'll] know how to openly express [your] commitments to purity and . . . fears of the consequences of premarital intimate contact. Second, young lovebirds usually choose between talk and the back seat. They don't do both simultaneously."[1]

If you truly desire to live a lifestyle of purity, you'll learn the secret of speaking boldly.

Load Your Lap with Tennis Balls

Wolgemuth was taking his young daughters to a friend's home for dinner one evening when a conversation skill he had heard James Dobson mention came in handy. Similar to pre-date jitters, the girls found themselves nervous about what to say and how to act. He told them to fill their laps with tennis balls before they sat down for dinner and be ready to throw them at their new friends. I am sure the girls' eyes were as wide as tennis balls when their dad announced they'd be throwing balls at the dinner table, but he went on to explain. The tennis balls were really questions, and when their new friends answered, it would be like another tennis ball coming back to them that needed to be caught. Then the girls could decide if it was a good ball that needed to be thrown back or if it was a bad one . . . in which case they would pick up a new question from

"a new question"

their lap and toss it out.[2] It's a great concept. Do you have a lap full of tennis balls for your dates?

What Hollywood Won't Tell You About Sex, Love and Dating, a book written by Greg Johnson and Susie Shellenberger, has a great chapter entitled "Dolt or Volt: Can You Carry on a Conversation?" The main difference between a "dolt" and a "volt" is that a "dolt" waits to be asked questions and a "volt" asks them. The chapter is full of good questions to ask, including:

- What are your favorite sports to play?
- What kind of car would you like to have? Why?
- Who are your heroes? Why?
- What are your top three memories of your grandparents?[3]

There are more. So grab a copy of the book and use them.

Another great way to get questions is to go back to your dream list that you should have written in chapter 7. This is your chance to find out if he is worth the ink on that list!

- So, what do you wanna be when you grow up?
  (Look for that compatibility in goals and dreams.)
- What's your mom like?
  (A man is often looking for a wife who is similar to her!)
- How involved are you in your church?
  (A good nonthreatening look at his commitment to the Lord.)

- Tell me about your relationship with God.
  (Better if you think he's got a good chance of being great for God.)

Watch the Foul Lines

I'm using this illustration of tennis balls, or conversation balls, as a great way to encourage you to speak boldly. But any great ball game has boundaries, and if the ball moves outside of the boundaries, you foul or you lose control of the ball. You need to watch the foul lines in your communication, as well.

By now you can tell that I was a little old-fashioned in my dating because I was confident that some old-fashioned dating was not only safe for the heart and the body, but it also drives a guy's heart right into a girl's hands. So, in honor of our last chapter . . . you need to set some guidelines about what you will and will not discuss. For me it was rather simple. I had determined two foul lines and one "technical."

Foul line 1

I will not discuss marriage to him until he romantically and lovingly makes the commitment to ask me to marry him.

I wanted the fairy tale and that included a bended knee, so I was determined not to spoil it by stealing the moment too early in any relationship. My husband and I did talk about marriage before we were engaged, but in a general sense and after we'd been dating for a good year and a half. We discussed things like how many children we each dreamed of having one day or what kind of home we hoped to own. They were all very general discussions, and the focus was on his dreams or my dreams, but never *our* dreams.

Foul line 2

I will not discuss sex, physical contact, or my physical desires with him.

A few months ago, I took a college-bound friend of mine to St. Louis for the day. She confided that she and her boyfriend struggled physically, so they talked about it . . . in detail. How her body felt. How his responded. What she desired. What he dreamed of. As soon as I got home, I grabbed one of my hip friends Donna and said, "Did you and your husband ever talk about your desires when you were dating?" "No way," she answered. "That would have made it far too difficult not to fulfill them and, in fact, would have been way sexier than actually fulfilling them."

Please, oh please, remember the power of your tongue. There is scientific evidence that the brain is the greatest of all sexual organs. Special chemicals are released within your brain to cause you to desire sexual activity, and they are released by sight and by conversation. So determine not to talk about your desires, as it will make it very difficult to control them.

This is also confirmed biblically. In the Song of Solomon, the Bible's great love story, the two lovers used passionate, loving words to awaken desires. Talk is intimate. If you are convinced that the relationship you are in is the godly dream that you have written about in your list and you have determined that you are ready to be married, pursue this person with lots of talk. Just take care what you talk about.

Avoiding a technical offense
I will communicate a desire to live a lifestyle of purity.

If you are caught "traveling" in basketball, you lose control of the ball. If you have a "hand ball" in soccer, you lose the ball. Technical offenses cause you to lose control of the game, and you have to work extra hard to regain your offensive position. You end up playing defense. I had determined that I was not going to commit the "technical" of failing to communicate my desire to live a lifestyle of purity. I was going to stay on the offense.

Mostly, this is communicated nonverbally, in the way that you dress, where you will go on a date, and the simple body cues you offer. But there may be occasions when it

Loose Lip Contract

I will keep my lips loose on a date. I commit to do the following:

I will begin each dating relationship with a "tennis-ball" load of questions.

Once I have found someone who meets my "dream" list, I will date him using these guidelines for conversation . . .

💜

I will not discuss marriage to him until he romantically and lovingly makes the commitment to ask me to marry him.

💜

I will not discuss sex, physical contact, or my desires with him.

💜

I will communicate a desire to live a lifestyle of purity.

_____
SIGNATURE

_____
DATE

needs to be communicated more blatantly.

I heard every word Bob Gresh *did not speak* to me that night when he said, "This is as far as I want our relationship to go." He was saying, "This is hard for me. I physically yearn for more, but I need you to hold me accountable to my desire to live a lifestyle of purity." Previously, I had made my own desire for purity known by playfully saying things like, "We kiss too much. I've got brains too, ya know." And, "Do you want to get to know me or my lips?" That put the end to our foolish beginning and got us headed toward something great.

Confessing your wish to be pure does two things: (1) It creates accountability to each other to live up to it and (2) it sets the standard. Notice that in my confrontation to Bob there was little detail as far as the desires that were awakened, and we were of marrying age.

Commit to communicate this nonverbally as you are "governed by your value" and seek to "speak boldly," but if the need or occasion arises, be prepared to draw the line quickly and with little detail about your physical desires.

Controlling the tongue is not easy. Since the tongue is so powerful, I'd like you to review by signing the contract for your lips on page 99!

Keep reading because the next secret proved to be the most crucial one to assure me a satisfying marriage.

Write Your Story

It's time to commit. Your lips are very powerful. You need to make a commitment with the loose lips contract, *but only if you intend to stick to it.* If you feel that you have failed in one of these four areas, take your journal out and write about it. Then, commit right here and now by signing the loose lip contract.

it's your
turn

Calling a Spade a Spade

"Let's be candid with ourselves before God. Call a spade a spade or even a muddy shovel. If your passions are aroused, say so—to yourself and to God, not to the object of your passion. Then turn the reins over to God. Bring your will to Him. Will to obey Him; ask for His help. He will not do the obeying for you, but He will help you. Don't ask me how. He knows how. You'll see."[4]

Top Ten Comeback Lines

OK, things have gone too far. He is reaching for the forbidden fruit . . . or maybe you are. It is time to say, "Freeze." What words will you use to do it? Below I have given you two of the best comeback lines I have heard in my retreats. You determine what other eight you will add to your list.

10. Isn't it cool that God is watching us every minute?

9. Hey, have I told you that my father dusts me for fingerprints when I get home from a date?

8. _____

7. _____

6. _____

5. _____

4. _____

3. _____

2. _____

1. _____

E-mail me your "Top Ten Comeback Lines." I may be able to list them for other girls at my retreats. My e-mail address is dannah@teameikon.com.

NOTES
1. Robert Wolgemuth, *She Calls Me Daddy* (Colorado Springs: Focus on the Family Publishing, 1996), 73.
2. Ibid., 62.
3. Greg Johnson and Susie Shellenberger, *What Hollywood Won't Tell You About Sex, Love and Dating* (Venture: Regal, 1994), 57-63.
4. Elisabeth Elliot, *Passion and Purity* (Grand Rapids: Revell, 1984), 96.

secret 5

PURITY
LOVES ITS
CREATOR AT
ANY COST

pursuing

a love

relationship

with Jesus

 secret 5

PURITY LOVES
ITS CREATOR
AT ANY COST

Pursuing a Love Relationship with Jesus

*The kingdom of heaven is like a merchant looking for
fine pearls. When he found one of great value, he
went away and sold everything he had and bought it.*
(MATTHEW 13:45-46)

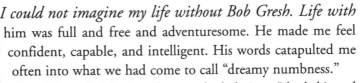*I could not imagine my life without Bob Gresh. Life with*
him was full and free and adventuresome. He made me feel
confident, capable, and intelligent. His words catapulted me
often into what we had come to call "dreamy numbness."
But this week I had made some bad choices. I had skipped
an important yearbook meeting when Bob had called at the
last minute to take me to Wittenberg Library. Instead of looking
up the Bible verses when the pastor encouraged us to do so in church, I
had opted to keep holding Bob's big, warm hand. And my roommate, Kimberly
Sweet, had given me a kind confrontation about how I was allowing my friendship with Bob to squeeze out my friendship with her and just about everyone
else. Our last few dates had included some passionate kissing. My journal had
become full of him and not God. After a year and a half of "pure, slow burning," I was beginning to slowly ease my way back into "crash and burn" mode.

So here I was in his apartment standing awkwardly near the door.

"Come in," he encouraged.

"I can't," I said as a tear slipped down my cheek and my lip began to quiver.
He had never seen me cry. He quickly began to move toward me with his arms
outstretched.

"No, don't," I softly demanded. "Listen to what I have to say first."

He stopped with the sofa the only object seemingly holding us from each other's arms.

"I treasure our friendship," I began. "I know that you do too. But we have got to be more in each other's spiritual lives than just someone to sit next to in church."

The look in his eyes told me he understood. I was not telling him we could not go on *like this*. I was not suggesting to him that we could change it. I was telling him we could not go on.

Our eyes never lost the intent, direct gaze as tears flooded our faces. Desperately wanting to hold each other, but knowing that might lead to more easy choices, we stood staring into each other's pain. After a long silence, he spoke.

"I know," he whispered, and we continued looking at each other hopelessly. I prayed silently for strength to carry through as my heart felt as if it was physically ripping within me and my body felt as if huge boulders were suddenly pushing me toward the floor.

"Oh, God," I said in my head. "I have never sacrificed something to You that I hold so dear. I don't know if You will give him back to me, but I will trust You to fill this huge void in my heart someday, somehow. Please, let it be him. Please, my dear Jesus."

After nearly a half hour of standing there in the silence of our pain and listening to the clock tick, I turned and quietly opened the door and left. I did not know if the door to this precious relationship would ever be opened again.

I know only one thing that is free, and that is God's loving forgiveness. But that short parable that Jesus told about the merchant and the pearl of great price says that to really pursue God, know God, and love God may require selling all that you have. God asks that we trade in all the fake pearls of our life to buy the real pearl. He says in Luke 14:33 that "any of you who does not give up everything he has cannot be my disciple."

In my retreats, I give the girls who attend a price tag that says "Everything costs something. Some things cost everything." We hear and tell testimonies about the cost of "fake pearls" in our lives.

Heidi, a pastor's daughter in her mid-twenties, told about how her vibrant, wonderful relationship with her dad—a rare treasure these days—is blocked by a deep secret. She became sexual with a guy she "really loved" and then he dumped her. In a heart-breaking, tear-stained night she confessed it to the guy who is now her loving husband, but she cannot bring herself to tell her dad. It hurts that she has not told him because they are so close. But she knows that telling him one day, which she plans to do, will also bring incredible pain.

One girl, Kylie, told how she hated the label of being "innocent" so she started being flirtatious to be more fun. One of her good friends stopped her and said, "I miss innocent Kylie. I liked her better. She was real." Kylie left the retreat knowing she was going to have to set some things straight and it was not going to be easy. In fact, she was expecting it to cost her some friendships.

Mikayla had been running with some girls in her youth group with bad attitudes. They joked around and took lightly the things of God. Right before I conducted a retreat at her church, she began to experience real spiritual revival in her life. Then she and her friends came to the retreat. As she melted into God's arms at the retreat, her friends began to get nervous. In bed, they cruelly taunted her and teased her as others watched. Running with the wrong crowd was costing Mikayla something as she began to make right choices.

The costs of "fake pearls" can be great. Giving your body away might someday need to be paid for in the form of pregnancy, AIDS, or some other STDs. Giving your

Today's Pearls

Want a great contemporary take on the pearl of great price? Pick up a copy of Jeni Varnadeau's CD "Colors of Truth" and listen to "Father Knows Best." I was working on this chapter and preparing to present it at a retreat for the first time when a friend stopped in for a quick visit. I told her about what I was working on, and she said, "I've got a great song for you to listen to!" She brought it by that afternoon, and I started to cry when I heard it. It is powerful, but you really have to hear it music and all.

(I don't think it was just a coincidence that my friend stopped in that day, do you?)

♥

Steven Curtis Chapman on the Cost of Following Christ

Dannah: One of my favorite songs of yours is "For the Sake of the Call." It talks about the cost of following Christ. As I listen to the song, I wonder, what inspired you to write that?

Steven: I found myself at a point spiritually of just being. I wanted to go deeper into the place where it begins to become a fire. I didn't want to go through the motions. What would that cost me to really do that? Does it only mean

(continued on page 109)

heart away could end in heartbreak and spiritual anemia.

Even seemingly "good" things can be fake pearls if they haven't had time to be cultured into the real thing. My relationship with Bob was like that. So we "sold" it to pursue God's best. The cost was great. During our breakup Bob's journal had many entries like this . . .

My dearest Dannah, being without you takes a lot of getting used to. Since this is my journal let me be completely honest. There is a large part of me that doesn't miss you right now; a large part that feels no emotions, no loss. However, there is also a large part of me that feels tremendous loss, almost a loss of hope. . . . There seems to be no life without you, Dannah. I have come to depend completely upon you. The absence of deep roots of God in my life is an unexplainable mystery. My heart is deceitful and desperately wicked. I am the least and yet there is hope. Sad thing is that I can't envision it anymore. The light has gone out. It is dark.

Love, Bobby

I never saw that journal entry until we were engaged. But I had written several much like it.

9-27-87. . .
God is sovereign. Jesus is enough. Those are my spiritual goals. The day I believe in them completely is the day I am ready for a relationship. That day seems so far away. Lord, give me patience.

10-10-87. . .
My head knows the path that I must take, but my heart is one tough muscle. Today in chapel Joseph Stowell said, "God will not do by miracle what I am to do by obedience." I sure wish He could do this by miracle. Obeying is very painful.

1-19-88. . .
"Thou wilt keep him in perfect peace, whose mind is stayed on thee . . ." Isaiah 26:3 (KJV)

Tonight I write only what God is saying to me . . . not out of fear that someone would read what I feel in my heart, but rather because I am afraid to articulate feelings I might have to destroy.

Today, those journal entries are proof of how much our relationship was more important to us than our God and of how we were sacrificing something precious so that our relationship with God could be our most priceless possession.

On December 6, I attended a Sunday school class taught by Bob. We were still not together, but my heart was healing and becoming stronger in the Lord. In the class, he read Matthew 13:45–46 which says, "The kingdom of heaven is like a merchant looking for fine pearls. When he found one of great value, he went away and sold everything he had and bought it." His journal from the night before outlined his message that day.

(from page 108)

I don't go to R-rated movies or don't have sex before marriage? What does it mean to be called a lover of Christ? I was asking God to show me the answer to what the cost was. I realized it does cost something. It costs everything. Why would I hold on to other people's expectations of me . . . like popularity? I am willing to sacrifice those things to live in God's way. In really understanding and being willing to pay the price, I wrote that song. It's funny, on the heels of "For the Sake of the Call," I wrote "The Great Adventure." I realized that this is the reward for the cost—we enter into the adventure that our life was created for.

The Lord has taught me much in reading His Word tonight. They can be summed up in five statements:

1. There is a pearl of great price.
2. We are to seek it.
3. We are commanded to purchase it.
4. It costs us everything.
5. It is worth the price.

I must come to the point where I stop the payments on the fake pearls in my life and start making the payment on the real pearl.
God costs everything. He is worth the price.

Bob had come to realize that if he wasn't willing to relinquish all the fake pearls in his life, he would never fully understand the full blessing of God's goodness.

Giving up each other had been such a portrait of that verse in our lives. I had watched so many of my girlfriends return from Thanksgiving break with huge engagement rings on their fingers. I smiled through my pain and congratulated them. I had many lonely, quiet Friday and Saturday nights. I had to confess my negligence to several friends and ask them to let me back into their lives. Bob and I had several classes together that quarter, and seeing him every day only resurfaced the pain I had worked at alleviating in my prayers.

During that time, my theme was "God is sovereign. Jesus is enough." Until I felt that in my heart, I had determined not to date Bob or anyone else.

Write Your Story

What are the fake pearls in your life? Please believe me that the sacrifice of them is worth the cost. What God can give you is so much more valuable. Take a moment right now to write a love letter to God and admit to Him what fake pearls you are clinging to with your lifestyle. Be honest and tell Him that there is a part of you that treasures these fake pearls and you really find it hard to surrender them. But trust Him to replace them with something far better. Now would be a good time to stop and do this.

it's your **turn**

Eleven days after Bob taught that Sunday school class on the pearl of great price, I went to my mailbox to find an envelope with my name scrawled in his handwriting. In it, he wrote

> *Matthew 13:45–46*
> *"The kingdom of heaven is like a merchant looking for fine pearls. When he found one of great value, he went away and sold everything he had and bought it."*
>
> *He costs everything. He is worth the price.*
>
> *You cost everything. You're worth the price.*

I did not realize it, but he had begun to understand that there would be one relationship between him and a woman, which was a portrait of the condition of his love for God. He was having a hard time waiting, but he was sending me some of his desire that I might wait along with him for God to culture us. We both had a lot of loving to do in our relationship with God before we would be ready to love each other. We continued the long process of waiting.

Months went by, yet we did not feel God's release to be together.

secret 6

PURITY
EMBRACES
WISE
GUIDANCE

CHAPTER TWELVE

inviting

your

parents

into your

love life

secret 6

PURITY
EMBRACES
WISE GUIDANCE

Inviting Your Parents into Your Love Life

 *"Lisa, my mom is going to call me tonight,"* I said as I walked out the door, a load of laundry under one arm.

"Did she tell you that?" asked Lisa, seeing the mischief in my eye.

"No, but she will call," I said with certainty. Lisa was running down the hall minutes later to get me from the laundry room. After a few moments of encouragement across the miles, we hung up and I grabbed my journal.

10-18-87... *1 Thessalonians 3 says that Paul sent Timothy to encourage the afflicted church. Kind of like my mom encouraging her afflicted daughter. I love her so much.*

My mom had just endured two days of travel with a wild-eyed freshman to and from Pennsylvania and Ohio. She had stayed for two nights in a guys' apartment where she deemed the highest nutrient value to be found in the ring of the bathtub rather than any boxed food in the kitchen. She'd done it for me. Because my heart was hurting and it made me feel valued. I went to bed that night feeling so loved.

The next morning after my 9:00 class, I walked with Lisa to the "Po," as we called the Cedarville College Post Office. It was a welcomed treat of the day.

Everyone hoped there might be a pink "You have a package waiting" card or a note from a special someone. On this particular day, I recognized the sloppy handwriting indicating that my special someone was my high school brother, Darin. True to reputation, the card itself was humorous but its purpose was to encourage me during this season of waiting. Under his name he had taken time to write, "I bet you are like a proton surrounded by an entire galaxy of electrons with guys just waiting to get their turn to take you out."

It was the boost I needed today to stay in this place of waiting.

———— ❖ ————

Tim and Beverly LaHaye, authors of the most popular Christian sex book on the market, tell about a special moment on their youngest daughter's wedding day. As they drove her to the church, she leaned forward and said, "Mom and Dad, you can be proud of yourselves. You raised two daughters in Southern California, and both of us were virgins on our wedding day!" Probably a bit teary-eyed to begin with, the family drove to the church enjoying a downpour of joyful tears. The LaHayes are so proud that their daughters have no regrets.

No doubt, the LaHaye girls had moments when they did not like their parents' involvement in their dating. They had to endure their dad's "pre-date" interviews of their guy-friends, could not single date at all until they graduated from high school, and had to share a full itinerary with their parents prior to each date. I wish the same rigid involvement for you from your parents. I can see your eyes rolling now. Hang with me.

Embracing your mother and father's involvement in your dating—or at least accepting it—is a vital secret in your pursuit of a lifestyle of purity. I did not realize this until I began to minister to young women and saw a very specific pattern. Girls who were close to their families and closely monitored by their families, especially their fathers, had a special strength to live a lifestyle of purity. Girls who were not close to their families and were not closely monitored by their families, especially their fathers, had a bent toward sexual curiosity and activity. That is not true 100 percent of the time, but it is in the majority of cases.

Even if you are somewhat close to your parents, you may feel tied down by their rules and at odds with their preferences. That's OK. What you are going through is called "individuation" or simply becoming independent. But the danger is that you will try to pull away completely before you have the experience and wisdom to protect yourself. Your parents' rules are built upon love and a knowledge that you do not have. I want to encourage you, maybe convince you, to lean into their involvement. Of course there are the obvious reasons, like the fact that they probably know you better than you know yourself in some ways. They deserve to be honored just because God says they do. But I see two vital reasons to embrace your parents' involvement in your dating life specifically as it relates to the issue of purity.

Your Father Can Fill That Special Guy-Shaped Hole in Your Heart

I know a wonderful man who has an exceptionally close relationship with his two daughters. He told me that one day his teenage daughter was sitting on his lap when suddenly she asked, "Dad, why am I not totally boy-crazy like some of my friends? I mean, I like guys, but I don't seem to *need* them like some of my friends do."

Without hesitation, he answered her saying, "Because right now, I am doing everything I can to fill that guy-shaped hole in your heart. So you don't need a guy."

I like that answer.

Let me get right to the point. *Girls who lack a positive father/daughter relationship are very much at risk to be sexually active.* David Blakenhorn in a book entitled *Fatherless America* wrote, "Many studies confirm that girls who grow up without fathers are at much greater risk for early sexual activity, adolescent childbearing, divorce and a lack of sexual confidence."[1] I have seen this confirmed in many sources. In fact, in one study of the sex lives of 400 teenage girls, the girls actually admitted that they often "swapped sexual encounters for the fathering they felt they weren't getting."[2] I don't want to push too many statistics at you, but that's a little scary since many of you don't even have the privilege of living with a father in the same house and those who do live with a father often find that relationship frustrating.[3]

When I was small, my father and I were very close. I was his little dog-training companion, often traveling with him on weekend trips to dog shows. He called me Sally. (I have no idea why, but it was like our secret love language.) He was always pinching me as if he could not get enough of me. It was really a neat little relationship. When I hit seventh grade, it was like a great big wall went up between my dad and me. Some of it was his fault. Some of it was my fault. I became withdrawn and quiet in an effort to begin to build my own world. It was very painful for both of us. The worst of it lasted until I went away

Great Idea

Grab your mom and your dad. Tell them you are reading this great book and there is a chapter all about them. Ask them to read it with you and to talk about this chapter. It might just be a great new beginning for you, or it could make you closer than ever!

to college, when we both began to realize how very much we missed each other.

I think sometimes dads become afraid of their daughters' changing bodies and begin to feel awkward about how they communicate with their little girls. One author wrote, "How puzzling it must be for a girl who has been used to being daddy's little girl, to snuggling in her father's lap and being tucked in at bedtime, suddenly to find her father pulling away. 'You are too big for that now,' her mother or father tells her. Too big for family hugs? Too big for paternal love? 'It feels like you did something wrong,' one teenager explained when talking about how her father started distancing himself."[4]

I always hold a discussion about dads when I conduct my purity retreats. There are always girls throughout the room reduced to tears as they express the craving they have to be loved and adored by their dads, but they admit that they too have hit a wall. Most of them admit that they crave the manly love that a dad can offer.

You must crash through that wall sometime. It won't necessarily get easier, and you never stop desiring a loving relationship with your dad. Your relationship with your father is, perhaps, never as important to you as during the teen and early adult years when, for many, it seems to be so tough to enjoy.

I'll give you some practical ideas for that father/daughter relationship in a moment. While I am trying to convince you of the need to embrace your parents' involvement in your dating relationships, I'd like to tell you the special thing that your mom can bring to the table.

Your Mother Has the Ability to Vaccinate You!

You remember that little red lizard and the little monsters we talked about in chapter 6, "Purity Is a Process"? Well, I believe many times they are inherited. From the families of alcoholics are born alcoholics. From the families of liars are born liars. From the families of sex addicts are born sex addicts. Ask any Christian psychologist or counselor. They will tell you that they see this pattern every day. It is also present within the Bible. For example, we know that David had a weakness for women. His sin with Bathsheba led to more sin in the form of murder. Solomon, David's son to Bathsheba, carried on the family iniquity. Solomon had seven hundred wives and three hundred concubines. Many of them were "foreign" women who did not believe in God. God clearly told Solomon not to marry them. Solomon had the same tendency toward sexual sin that his father David displayed.

Look at it like this: When you were ever so small, your parents knew there were certain diseases that you could catch such as polio and German measles. Because these can be deadly or cause severe damage to you, they chose to take a tiny amount of this sickness and inject it into your perfect little body. They knew that if your body was aware of this disease, it could learn to fight it.

It is much the way with diseases of the soul. The same diseases or sins that your parents came up against in their life will very likely be the ones you struggle with as well. If you can be given a taste of that through their testimony— and perhaps seeing their shame and regret—you will be better able to fight against it.

So, how do you fix a rough relationship with your dad or mom? How do you get comfortable enough with your mom and/or dad to embrace their involvement in your dating life? It can be a long and difficult process, but I have a few simple ideas to get you started.

Write a Letter

One of the things that I have seen have a great impact is letter writing. I wrote many letters to both of my parents when I was in junior and senior high school. It always seemed to readjust both my attitude and their response to me. As I wrote, I often found that a lot of what I expected from them was selfish and demanding. I was able to go back through the letter and edit it before I gave it to them in final form. It was a good exercise in examining my own attitude. As I edited, only the legitimate concerns made it through to the end. With my selfishness out of the way, my parents were able to see my point, and we often came to a good understanding.

Ron Hutchcraft recommends this kind of communication too. He says that a letter is "usually better said, better heard, and better remembered." He has often seen a simple letter transform families.[5]

Writing a letter is something that I particularly recommend if you are struggling with your relationship with your dad. Even if you are not struggling with the relationship, it is vital that you pursue an open relationship with him. Won't you sit down right now and write a letter to your dad? Express to him how

Rebecca St. James on Dads

Dannah: What are some things you have done to strengthen the bond between you and your father?

Rebecca: It is kind of interesting that you ask about that. My dad and I are really close because we work together. He is my manager, and some have asked, "Well, isn't that strange working with your dad?" But I think it is really good because he really understands me and is looking out for my best interest even more than any manager ever could. There have been times where

(continued on page 121)

much you crave his affection. Maybe tell him some of what you have felt God telling you as you read this chapter. Tell him how vital the father/daughter relationship is for you. Tell him you love him. If the relationship is strained, tell him you feel hurt by the wall between you and ask him to be your hero and to come crashing through it to find you again. Go ahead. Give it a try. Recognize that your dad is a very important element in your journey to live a lifestyle of purity. Oh, you can do it without him, but it is easier with him walking beside you.

Look for Your Dad's Love Language

Men Are from Mars, Women Are from Venus was the title of one of the fastest selling relationship books in the past decade. Why did it sell so quickly? Because nearly every woman could identify with trying to talk to the man of her dreams and feeling as if he was talking in some language so foreign it had to be from another planet. Well, guess what? Dads and daughters have a hard time talking the same language too.

A wise friend of mine, who has raised three wonderful, now-grown children, told me this secret. She said that often when her husband and daughters communicated, the girls had a hard time seeing his love. So she taught them to look for his love language.

As soon as she told me this little secret, I could see my dad's love languages all over the place. He and I did not hug and kiss and touch a lot. We did not go on "dates." We were hardly ever alone for quiet talks, but he loved me in his way. When I turned in a science project in high school, it was always one of the best because my dad would spend hours and hours painting solar panels, photographing dogs' noses, or covering display boards in felt. If I called him from college with a question about how to study, he would talk forever. I had and still have this notion that my dad can fix absolutely anything I break because he always, always has.

You might not feel your dad's love. The fact is, you might never easily see it in the language that you would like him to speak. But look for it. Look hard. Don't expect him to try to speak your love language. Identify how he says "I love you" and accept it as his own unique love language.

Confide in Your Mother

I don't run into quite as many of you struggling with deep issues in regards to your mom. Probably the most frequent issue is that she might not be communicating as effectively as you might like. You may feel like she isn't *really* hearing you, especially on the issue of relationships. The majority of you have stated that you'd like to talk to her about issues of sex.[6] Although your mother is the parent who will be most likely to communicate with you about sex, the two of you often have a great big communication gap. In one study, 75 percent of the mothers felt like they were communicating very directly and effectively with their daughters when it came to sex. Only half of the daughters agreed.[7]

So, what's the problem?

While you are discovering, deciding, and searching for answers to your own issues of sexuality and purity, you are resurfacing the

(from page 120)

I felt like I wanted more from him, and I think sometimes I expect too much. Especially as I get older . . . I expect him to kind of give me that support that maybe what I am longing for is the love or support that will come from my future husband. Sometimes my expectations are too high. I have to be careful. But if my expectations are legitimate and I am not expecting too much, I go to him and be honest about how I am feeling. I say, "Dad, this is a need in me" or "Dad, you really hurt me when this happened." We just make up about it, but that's hard to do. 'Cause I revere my father and respect him so much, so sometimes I am a little scared of going to him like that. But I think it is really important to go to him when you've got that hurt like that.

♥

discovering, deciding, and searching she did when she was your age. She has been right where you are and knows exactly how you are feeling. She once struggled with waiting to give her heart to someone just like you are waiting right now. It is never easy, but it could be easier for you if you lean into her wisdom.

Your best bet at benefitting from her wisdom is to be honest with her about the level of emotional and physical involvement you have with guys. (Hopefully not much if you aren't of marrying age!) I say that cautiously because each mother/daughter pair will be different, and you might have a mother who is really hard to talk to on this level. But don't assume that will be the case—try it. I am confident that most mothers would feel blessed for their daughters to confide in them about their dating life. When it comes to communicating about sex and dating, remember that purity speaks boldly. This is a good time to put that into practice. Tell her where you are. You might be surprised at what it will do.

I wish I had done this much earlier with my mother. I was probably seventeen when I really started to ask her advice about guys. My mother and I are both "pleasers." That can make the dating thing tough. I spent hours talking with my mom to help me make it through my craving to give my heart to Bob during the long season that God called me to give it to Him. During that time she told intimately how she struggled with many of the same things and what the cost of giving in to that struggle turned out to be years later. It gave me a resolve to carry on with the pure, slow burn. I absolutely could not have done it without her, and I desperately wished I had embraced her wisdom and advice years earlier.

With my mom's incredible patience and guidance, I managed to wait a long time for God to strengthen my love for Him. When God did finally give Bob and me a release to be together again, it was unbelievably worth the wait.

"Are you feeling OK?" I asked Bob.

"Yeah," he answered unconvincingly.

We sat in H&R Dairy eating burgers and fries. Well, I was eating. He was gagging with every bite of his french fries. His burger sat getting cold.

I was glad that our friendship was back on track. It was a sweet gift from God, which we had waited painfully to receive. I still longed for so much more, but at least we had both felt the release to be together again, and over the course of the past few months we had built some of our best memories. We'd had to

CHAPTER TWELVE **123**
secret #6: purity embraces wise guidance

change tires in the rain on our way to his Junior/Senior Banquet in Cincinnati. We'd had lots of long, intimate talks in Wittenberg Library. He'd taken me to Yellow Springs and spent the afternoon photographing me like I was a model. He was everything I had dreamed of and hoped for, in part because waiting at God's feet had made him more patient, more sensitive, and more romantic. (That was a definite plus!)

I was afraid of the next few months though. Tomorrow he would graduate. Monday he would start a job and would be a bachelor living eight hours away from me while I took another year to finish college. Oh, it felt like the waiting was going to start all over again.

One hour later, I was looking back across the audience of about two thousand college students and parents in Cedarville College's chapel. My friend Donna Payne had told me that Bob's "Senior Night," the dramatic stroll down memory lane that was a tradition the night before graduation, was highly formal. She'd convinced me to wear my soft silk dress, but I couldn't see a stitch of silk, lace, or anything close to formal in the house.

The lights went low and I watched as the class of 1988 portrayed some of their funniest moments. Then, out on the stage came Bob with Christine.

Wait a minute, I thought. My heart started pounding as I thought to myself, *He was supposed to be on costume duty. I didn't think he had an onstage part.*

They made small talk and then . . .

"Well, Bob, when are you gonna pop the question?" asked Christine.

"The question?" he answered nervously. That french fry gag seemed to be still getting the worst of him.

"Yeah," she pushed. "You and Dannah have been together a long time. Don't you think it's about time?"

My heart started pounding so loudly within me that I was certain everyone in my row could feel the vibration.

"Yeah, yeah," he said casually. "It is about time, but I had always dreamed of asking her somewhere with lots of friends and maybe even family present. You know, share in this great moment of joy. I'd want it to be just perfect."

"Well," she pushed, "why don't you show me what your version of just perfect would be like?"

"First," he answered as she faded offstage. "I'd look into my pocket to see if I had the ring." He pulled a black velvet box from his pocket as the audience rustled in awe.

"Then, I'd look for her in the audience," he said, walking off the stage toward me.

"Then, I'd take her by the hand," he said as he reached for me. As he walked me to the stage, I felt as if I was floating behind him. As I reached the stage there was a chair in front of me, which I collapsed into since my knees seemed to have forgotten how to bend. He kneeled before me and looked into my eyes. Then he presented the box and opened it. The spotlights caused the diamond, which was surrounded by six beautiful sapphires, to glisten against the black velvet.

"Dannah Barker," he asked. "Will you marry me?"

Silence.

Time stopped.

His eyes.

His smile.

His heart laid so humbly before me.

It was my line and I knew what to say, but the emotion of this moment was welling up within me. How could I speak?

"Oh, yes," I exploded with a smile and a giggle as our emotions were quenched in a strong embrace. As we walked offstage, the audience went wild, adding joy to this moment. I noticed for the first time members of my family and his, beaming with joy from the corner. Their cheers, encouragement, and wisdom had brought us to enjoy this most beautiful moment with them. It was a moment that could not be ruined or robbed by poor choices. The pure, slow burn had paid off. My prince was here and the sunset was creeping up over the horizon. April 29, 1989, was soon determined to be the day that we would ride off into it.

NOTES

1. David Blakenhorn, *Fatherless America* (New York: Basic Books, 1995), 46.
2. Kristine Napier, *The Power of Abstinence* (New York: Avon Books, 1996), 67.
3. Ibid., 19.
4. Nathalie Bartle, *Venus in Blue Jeans* (Boston: Houghton Mifflin, 1998), 172.
5. Ronald Hutchcraft, *How to Get Your Teenager to Talk to You* (Wheaton, Ill.: Victor, 1984), 50.
6. Napier, *Power of Abstinence,* 9.
7. Bartle, *Venus,* 97.

THE
TRUTH
**ABOUT
SEX: IT'S**
OUT OF
THIS
WORLD

CHAPTER THIRTEEN

understanding

the heavenly

purpose

of sex

THE TRUTH
ABOUT SEX:
IT'S OUT OF
THIS WORLD

Understanding the Heavenly Purpose of Sex

*"I present my body as a living sacrifice that is holy
and acceptable. This is only reasonable in light of
what You have done for me!"*
(RESPONSE TO ROMANS 12:1)

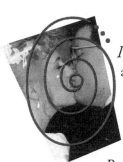

I lay with my body wedged into my new husband's, amazed
at the gift of our first experience together. It was tender and
fulfilling, proof of our love. It was awkward and unperfected,
proof of our innocence. Never, in all my life, had I felt this
warm and comforted as if the world had stopped around me
simply so that I could really know and feel this moment.

Bob began to move away from me.

"No, don't go," I murmured, drawing him back to me.

He turned and kissed me tenderly on my nose, then proceeded to get out
of bed. He tenderly and tightly wrapped me in the blankets and then knelt
beside me.

"Dannah, I want to pray," he said. "I want to thank God for this gift and
beg His blessing upon our marriage bed that we might always protect it."

There in the night with the moonlight shining a ray of light across our
honeymoon bed, we praised the great God of the universe for our wedding night.

How can I even start to rearrange the meaning of sex in your mind? What
you are exposed to on a daily basis is destructive to sex as God intended it to
be. And much of what you see isn't even close to reality. The average person

between the ages of two and eighteen sees 14,000 sexual references, innuendoes, and jokes each year on television. Fewer than 175 of those deal with the real issues of pregnancy/birth control, abstinence, or sexually transmitted diseases. On the most popular evening shows that most teenagers watch, the conversation deals with sex 29 to 59 percent of the time, with *Beverly Hills 90210* being at the low end of that scale. *Friends* and *Dawson's Creek* are also loaded with sexual references but watched by many Christian young people. On soap operas sex is twenty-four times more common between unmarried partners than between spouses.[1] Sex is the most frequently used search word on the Internet, and even if you don't search using that word, you are likely to run into sexual content. President Bill Clinton started an open debate about whether or not *some* sexual contact is actually sex at all. The world makes sex seem common, casual, and cheap.

Yet we don't hear much in church or private religious schools about how beautiful and honored sex is in God's eyes. Ed Young wrote,

> *Based on what is depicted by the media, any alien visitor to America would likely conclude that every person over the age of twelve is sexually active, that marriage is the last place to look for sexual satisfaction, that faithfulness is a nostalgic dream, and that even the sickest of sexual perversions is nothing less than every citizen's "inalienable right."*

> *This would be true, of course, unless they happened to visit the church. Then they would probably wonder whatever became of sex. They might never hear it mentioned at all—or perhaps only spoken of in whispers or condemning tones. Historically, to its shame, the church has either ignored the God-given gift of human sexuality or smothered it with an avalanche of "Thou shalt nots."[2]*

Stop right now. Quietly invite the Holy Spirit to reveal to you the truth of what my hands have typed. The truth that I am about to reveal to you is powerful, but not often spoken of . . . even in our churches. I want you to see it through God's eyes. Please stop to pray earnestly for God to speak to you.

Within the Scriptures, there are only four blood sacrifices. Before Christ came, God was honored and people showed repentance by the blood sacrifice of animals. And when God made His covenant with Abraham, He requested pain and blood through circumcision as an act of good faith on Abraham's part. By cutting away his foreskin, he demonstrated that his heart had gone through a change. (Ouch!) Those are the first two blood covenants.

The third and most magnificent is the atoning blood of Jesus, which is God's covenant to us that if we confess our sins, He is willing to erase them. (Thank You, Jesus!) The blood covenant of Jesus replaces the need to sacrifice animals and the need to practice male circumcision. Circumcision is still widely practiced, but mostly as a matter of cleanliness and health.

But wait, before you think, "Whew, I am glad I don't live in Bible times and have to practice animal sacrifice!" There is one left that God still asks us to practice! It was in existence in the Old Testament under the Law, but in the New Testament it has new meaning and is the only blood covenant sacrifice God still asks that we practice today. My friend, it is your sexuality.[3]

In Bible times, a bride and groom were presented with white linens for their wedding night. They were expected to sleep on them, and the bride was expected to bleed on them as proof of her virginity. You see, God created you and me with a protective membrane, the hymen, which *in most cases* is broken the first time that we have intercourse. When it breaks, a woman's blood spills over her husband.

Your sexual union is a blood covenant between you, your husband, and God.

In the Old Testament, Malachi 2:14–15 warns us not to break the covenant of marriage. God asks us to prize our virginity and hold it up as our only blood covenant to Him. Revelation 21:9 calls Christians "the bride, the wife

What Is a Covenant?

The word covenant *is taken lightly these days. It is often compared to a contract, but a covenant is far more than a contract. You see, when we enter into a covenant with God, we are receiving the gifts He grants (such as sexual pleasure, unity, and the blessing of children in marriage) based upon our faithfulness to the covenant. We are also agreeing that if we break that covenant (like many do when they divorce or commit adultery), that we will lose the full blessings of that covenant. A covenant is an if/then agreement. If you are faithful to it, then you will experience the full joy of it. You cannot expect to know the full blessings of it unless you commit to it with all of your heart. Expect the fullest of blessings from your marriage covenant, my friend. Know that on your wedding day it is an unbreakable covenant, and purpose to be faithful to it.*

The Hymen

The hymen is named after the mythical god of marriage. It's a tiny little membrane, which surrounds but does not entirely enclose the lower opening of your vagina. The hymen has no known function and never grows back after it has been dilated or torn. In some very rare instances, a baby girl is born without one or a young girl's hymen can be torn through rigorous exercise or accidents.[4] Let's pretend that it never, ever existed. This does not erase the physical portrait that the sexual union portrays of the spiritual truth of Christ and His beloved church.

of the Lamb [Jesus]." Before Jesus was ever born to Mary, the Jewish marriage customs were a portrait of Christ's relationship to us—that is, those who have embraced Him as Lord and Savior.

When a young Jewish man had his eye on a bright-eyed Jewish girl, he went with his father to her father. At that meeting, the groom-to-be was expected to present some sort of payment for the bride. A cow or two, some currency of the day, or a promise of labor were some of the forms of payment. If the father of the girl found the payment acceptable, he agreed that the young man could have his precious daughter *if* he first prepared a home for her. Off the young man went to grab his hammer and some lumber. He built a separate home if he could afford it. If not, he added a special section to his father's home for himself and his new bride.

During the time that this young man was building, the bride had a special job to do. She was expected to be waiting. Oh, not just going about her everyday chores and thinking about her groom-to-be. No, she was expected to be *waiting!* She was expected to have as lovely a dress as she could make or find by her side. She was to be cleaned and covered in aromatic oils. She was to be telling her friends of her groom's one-day arrival. At night, she was expected to have an oil lamp burning as a sign that she was faithfully waiting. The lamp *could not* go out. It was the sign that she was ready.

Her groom returned the moment he finished their home. There would be no delay. If it was 3:00 in the morning, so be it. He would sneak into her home with his friends, first checking to see if the oil lamp was burning. Then he awoke her and carried her through the streets shouting and rejoicing that she was ready and he could provide for her. The night would be one of solitude for the new   couple to consecrate their marriage, and then the sometimes weeklong celebrations began!

Do you see what I see? I know you must see how romantic this was, but do you see the portrait? Do you see Jesus coming to earth just like the young man first came to the young woman's house? Matthew 25:1–13 compares the way that the church waits for Christ to the way a virgin faithfully waits for her husband. Can you see Him paying for our lives with His blood on the cross like the young man paid the father? Do you recall His ascending into heaven where He went to "prepare a place" for you and me, much like the young man went to build the house for his bride? And someday, when we least expect it, Jesus will return for His church in all of His glory and those who call Him Savior will be with Him forever, like the groom came

PHOTO COURTESY OF T. AND H. SMITH

"the marriage covenant is an if/then agreement"

back to take his virgin bride to live with him for the rest of their lives. Yes! I love the romance of the Jewish wedding tradition, but I love the powerful symbolism even more.

Ed Wheat, a physician, wrote,

> *The sex relationship receives such emphasis in the Scriptures that we begin to see it was meant not only to be a wonderful, continuing experience for the husband and wife, but it also was intended to show us something even more wonderful about God and His relationship with us. Ephesians 5:31, 32 [KJV] spells it out: "For this cause shall a man leave his father and mother, and shall be joined unto his wife, and they two shall be one flesh. This is a great mystery, but I speak concerning Christ and the church." Thus, the properly and lovingly executed and mutually satisfying sexual union is God's way of demonstrating to us a great spiritual truth. It speaks to us of the greatest love story ever told—of how Jesus Christ gave himself for us and is intimately involved with and loves . . . those who believe in him.[5]*

Oh, do you see what God has entrusted to you? The young bride who enters into her marriage a faithful virgin can celebrate wholeheartedly. (And I am not just talking about technical virginity. I am talking about a pure virgin whose mind is as pure as her body.) What great joy to be able to enter into a covenant relationship with a man on your wedding night with no memory of having that covenant marred! I cannot think of any greater earthly joy.

Perhaps you feel a bit left out because you do have some memories that will be tough to erase on that night. Well, my friend, I share that pain. I cannot say that the consequences have not been quite hurtful, but I can say that we serve a loving God who can mend every broken heart. If this truth hurts, I am sorry, but please keep reading and know that God is forgiving. I have some special encouragement for you at the end of the next chapter.

Covenants within Scripture were always "if-then" agreements. *If* Abraham would practice the covenant of circumcision, *then* he would be blessed with a great legacy of generations that followed God. *If* Old Testament characters would practice the blood covenant of sacrificing animals, *then* God would see their faith and forgive their sins. *If* Jesus shed His blood for our sins and we accept and embrace Him as Savior, *then* we could be forgiven and someday enter into heaven. So, you're asking, what's the *then, if* we wait until our wedding night to share in the sexual union with just one man?

Read on, my friend, and see that His blessing back to us comes in the forms of three lovely gifts.

Write Your Story

In the Old Testament animal sacrifices were made for atonement and for praise. Today our bodies are to be *living* sacrifices (Romans 12:1–2). Stop a moment and read Psalm 63:1–8 and offer up your body as a sacrifice of praise to God. As David writes about each body part and praises God with it, give Him that part of you. Focus especially on verse 1 where he talks about

it's your **turn**

his flesh yearning for God. Pray that into your life to replace worldly passions. Take this time to praise Him with your purity!

NOTES
1. Nathalie Bartle, *Venus in Blue Jeans* (Boston: Houghton Mifflin, 1998), 104–5.
2. Ed Young, *Pure Sex* (Sisters, Oreg.: Multnomah, 1997), 18.
3. Edwin Louis Cole, *The Glory of Sex* (Tulsa: Honor Books, 1993), 35.
4. Ed and Gaye Wheat, *Intended for Pleasure* (Grand Rapids: Revell, 1977), 53.
5. Ibid, 22.

THE
TRUTH
ABOUT
SEX:
GETTING
DOWN TO
EARTH

CHAPTER FOURTEEN

preparing to

enjoy the

earthly gift

of sex

THE TRUTH
ABOUT SEX:
GETTING DOWN
TO EARTH

Preparing to Enjoy the Earthly Gift of Sex

Twenty of us sat in our pajamas in a circle with candles glowing at my purity retreat. God had given me this delightful opportunity to show girls how to make it to their wedding night without regret.

Jenny Ralls's cotton pj's looked as soft as her creamy, white complexion. Her dimples chiseled a bit deeper into her cheeks as she chattered on and on with delight. She was giving a fantastic testimony about how she came to her marriage bed a virgin—physically and mentally.

"I dated a guy for four years. He was sexually active frequently before we dated. And we even got engaged, but I told him I would not participate in that," she remembered, a sense of gratitude coming through in her voice. "The relationship brought a great deal of pain when he broke up with me. I felt like I was going to be an old spinster. One month after we broke up, he was in another sexual relationship," she said matter-of-factly.

She communicated her great sense of relief, but also a great deal of pain wondering what God could possibly have in store for her. Soon, she said, He brought Bryan into her path. Handsome, athletic, popular, and driven, Bryan was also a virgin. The relationship escalated quickly into a vibrant partnership for Jesus. Her love for singing and his love for playing the trumpet complemented each other.

*Becky Tirabassi
on Intimacy*

Dannah: Have you seen intimacy being enhanced as you and your husband both pursue a strong prayer life?

Becky: I feel that it is my quiet time that moves me from a place where I may have some past hurt, or pain, or blockage, or laziness, or selfishness, to a place where I want to meet my husband's needs. The longer I am married the less I make excuse for my past and consider that my immorality or my promiscuousness are the reasons that I am inhibited. My time with God clarifies who I am and enables me to meet my husband's needs almost unrelated to my past. I would just want to do that because I love him so much and he is such a neat guy!

"Someone got me a copy of a good Christian sex book right before we got married," said Jenny. "I'd read this and I was like, 'Wow! Oh, I cannot wait for this.' I can remember reading parts of it out loud to my mom and dad and asking questions. There was simply no shame. I could not wait!"

Jenny's bright eyes twinkled with extra brightness as she talked about her passion for Bryan. "You know, we just might be having really lousy sex, but we have nothing to compare it to, and so we have a blast together," she said with a giggle.

Somehow, I thought, *I am pretty sure that Jenny and Bryan have glorious sex, and I believe it is because God has blessed their marriage covenant.*

I truly believe that when we keep that covenant by saving ourselves to love someone with all the intensity of our heart and body, He is able to bless us immeasurably beyond what we could have imagined within our sex lives. Bryan and Jenny were living that to the fullest, and it showed in her glow.

Sex Is Great Fun!

Like Jenny said, God made sex to be pleasurable beyond your wildest dreams. Proverbs 5:18–19 says, "May your fountain be blessed, and may you rejoice in the wife of your youth. A loving doe, a graceful deer— may her breasts satisfy you always, may you ever be *captivated* by her love!" (italics added).

Captivated! I love that word. Don't you love the idea of being the object of one man's desire to the point of captivating him? Josh

McDowell told me that in the original language that verse read something more like this—"may you be intoxicated by her sex!" Whoa! So, that verse is all about being completely overtaken by the joy of sex with your spouse. God can do that for you. That blessing comes from being in God's presence and waiting for His timing for this gift of sexual union. Want proof?

In 1975, *Redbook* magazine published a survey conducted by Robert and Amy Levin. They took an in-depth look at the sex lives of 100,000 women. They labeled a portion of their respondents "strongly religious." "The strongly religious woman seems to be even more responsive than other women her age," they wrote. These women were more likely to experience "a higher degree of sexual enjoyment and greater frequency in love making experiences per month."[1]

On the contrary, those who fail to wait tend to face obstacles in learning to have fun in their married sex lives. In *What Hollywood Won't Tell You About Sex, Love and Dating,* Greg Johnson says that he and his wife were virgins by God's grace when they got married, but they had been physical up to a certain point. Because of that sexual activity, they had trained her body to get to that point and stop. So, when they got married, it took them several years of reconditioning to teach her body to enjoy sexual intimacy and get to the point where they were blessed by the fantastic fun of the sex.[2]

> "No good thing will he withhold from them that walk uprightly."
>
> (PSALM 84:11 KJV)

I am not saying that sex outside of marriage might not have some pleasurable moments. But it's a substitute for the real depth of pleasure that can be experienced within a faithful marriage, and it can really water down the pleasure you have with your husband.

God is waiting to fill you with more blessing than you can imagine. Don't miss how much fun sex can be. *If* you will wait, *then* it will be exciting!

Sex Is for Making Babies!

Giving birth was the single most fulfilling accomplishment of my entire life, and I have a hunch that it will not be equaled. I remember a particularly proud moment that came in a most humbling circumstance. One hour after my beautiful Alexis was born, I found myself naked in a shower being tenderly washed down by a nurse. It was wonderful. I felt so spoiled. (Everyone should get a sponge bath like this sometime in her life.) As the warm water trickled

*But what if you
have made some bad
choices in your past?*

*"Your disobedience does not
remove God from your life.
It does remove God's
blessing from your life."
My pastor, Tim Cook, said
that this past Sunday, and it
stuck. I realized that that
time when I was mired down
in a bad relationship, God
was still there. But He is
just and simply could not
bless me. Oh, how He
wants to bless us. And, oh,
how He did bless me when
I stood before Him and
begged for forgiveness
and healing.
Want a really exciting
example of how you
might be restored? Rahab!*

(continued on page 139)

down my body, I recounted every little pain and every big, "ouchy" push. I could hardly stay on the ground as the pride bubbled inside of me at the thought of a little girl to take home to my adored toddling boy. There was not one modest bone in my body at that moment. I remember wanting to open the door to invite everyone in for a peek and to scream, "Do you have any idea what *THIS* body just did! It is amazing!"

The God of the universe has given you the incredibly godlike gift of creating life. I don't think one person on this earth could actually begin to explain why or how one tiny round egg cell and one swimming sperm cell could turn into a vibrant life, but through the gift of sex it does happen.

Of course, you can make life whether or not you are in the covenant of marriage. But creating a life is the most incredible thing you will ever do. It deserves to be unmarred and undistracted by bad timing. *If* you will wait, *then* when you make new life, it will be with great celebration!

Sex Enhances Intimacy!

I must be perfectly honest with you—after ten years of marriage my husband and I don't have sex a lot. Mostly, between two wonderful, adorable (I-can't-wait-to-go-pick-them-up-today) kids, three businesses to run, a budding writing career (wow!), a great home to care for, a busy church family, and commitments to social needs, we get too tired to be crazy lovers. That is reality. Despite what Hollywood might try to tell you, most healthy, red-blooded humans do not engage in sex as often as they brush their teeth.

However, when my husband and I do enjoy the great gift of physical closeness, there is a difference in our relationship. We talk more. We help each other more. We hug more. We hate being apart. We can't wait to see each other again. We lie around and talk like we are college kids again. We dream. We confess. We laugh. We are consumed with each other as we go about our day, whether we are riding bikes with the kids, teaching a high school Bible study, or washing dishes. *We are one.*

Genesis 2:24 says that we should leave our father and mother and "be united" and become "one flesh."

That's hard to fathom, but couples who have purity within their marriage experience a distinct "oneness." What makes it even harder to understand is the casual approach to sex that much of today's social and political arena endorses.

Sadly, this gift is most at risk if you are sexual outside of marriage. In fact, I have frequently heard girls and guys talk about how sex outside of marriage really drove them apart rather than brought them together.

Plus, if you are sexually active before you are married, you may find yourself returning to memories with another sexual partner at a moment that should be for just you and your husband. What a sad thing to be robbed of those precious, private moments. Oh, guard yourself against that!

Intimacy starts with something in your heart, not with your body. But within the marriage relationship sex really enhances and

(from page 138)

You know, Rahab the prostitute! Rahab was one of the Canaanite people who were so sinful that God had condemned them to die. Her particular sin was sexual. But Rahab became a believer, and her life was spared when the land of Canaan was overtaken. But the story doesn't end there.

She married an Israelite and had a son named Boaz, who had a son named Obed, who had a son named David. See it yet? Jesus was born out of the line of David.

God saw Rahab's new, pure, clean life and claimed it to be in the family tree of Jesus Christ. Now that's a blessing! He wants to see you experience blessing in your life.

♥

Take It a Step Further!

Earlier, I mentioned a survey of 3,377 married couples by Tim and Beverly LaHaye. According to them, those couples who prayed together regularly were more than 10 percent more likely to have a "very happy/ above average" sex life than those who did not pray together.[4] Wow! God loves to be in the very center of a vibrant marriage relationship and He blesses that with the great physical gift of sexual satisfaction.

creates a new level of intimacy that can only be experienced between two fully committed, faithful, lifetime lovers.

In her effort to convince America to embrace abstinence and forget the safer sex message, Kristine Napier wrote, "Sex involves not just the sexual organs, but also the heart and mind. Teaching only the mechanics of sex and contraception ignores this. It ignores the concept that sexual intercourse is about total love and commitment, about sharing the singularly spectacular gift of oneself. . . . We must help [people] understand the human side of sex—the emotional and spiritual qualities that make it distinctly human."[3]

God loves to bless us. When we stay within the confines of His covenant, He loves to bless us in three ways.

If you will wait, *then* it will be a blast.

If you will wait, *then* you'll make babies with great celebration.

If you will wait, *then* you will be one. You will know a unity that few people have the privilege of tasting. You will understand the great mystery of how God can take two and make them one.

If you will wait . . .
then you will be blessed!

NOTES
1. Robert J. Levin and Amy Levin, "Sexual Pleasure: The Surprising Preferences in 100,000 Women," *Redbook* 145 (September 1970): 52.
2. Greg Johnson and Susie Shellenberger, *What Hollywood Won't Tell You About Sex, Love and Dating* (Venture: Regal, 1994), 17–18.
3. Kristine Napier, *The Power of Abstinence* (New York: Avon Books, 1996), 60–61.
4. Tim and Beverly LaHaye, *The Act of Marriage* (Grand Rapids: Zondervan, 1976), 209.

facing the

consequences

to find

healing

NOT YOU AGAIN, SATAN!

Facing the Consequences to Find Healing

"Psst! No one needs to know about this!"

14 God said to the snake, "Because you have done this, you are cursed more than any wild animal and you will crawl on your belly and eat dirt all the days of your life. 15 I will put hatred between you and the woman—between your seed and her Seed. He will crush your head though you only strike His heel." 16 And to Eve, God said, "You will have great pain in childbirth. And you will have an unquenchable desire for your husband who will rule over you." 17 To Adam he said, "Because you listened to Eve, I curse the ground that you will painfully work to feed yourself. 18 The ground will grow thorns and thistles for you and you will now have to eat the plants of the field. 19 By your sweat you will have food to eat until you die. From the ground I made you and now to the ground you will return." . . . 21 Then God made garments of skin for Adam and Eve and clothed them.

(GENESIS 3:14-19, 21, AUTHOR'S PARAPHRASE)

The lodge had been the perfect choice for this retreat. Pajamas, popcorn, and a hot tub were what I needed to leave behind the deadlines, management duties, and a dirty house. Within twelve hours, I'd bonded to many of the dear women as we were challenged to reach deep within ourselves and find those things in our lives that still hurt. As the facilitator began to draw things to a close in the final session, she invited women to practice the principle of release. She invited them to truly start healing by confessing long hidden secrets. After a few minutes of awkward silence one woman stood.

"I was sexually active before I was married. My husband doesn't know."

The tears flowed.

"I had an abortion. It felt like my soul would never heal. Then, I had another."

"I have been in and out of relationships since I was thirteen. I am totally dependent on men."

"I never told anyone, but my uncle abused me sexually."

The women drew closer and continued talking and encouraging for hours.

Embraces.

Tears.

Healing.

Freedom.

I was seeing active, godly, churchgoing women in their thirties, forties, and fifties admit the secret sins—sometimes not even their own sins—that were still causing great pain after decades. Many of them were confessing sexual sins. Most of them were dredging up memories from their teenage years. As the session turned into hours of talking, hugging, and crying, I watched the countenance on these women's faces change into relaxed contentment. They would leave released from the blackmail Satan had been using to ransom their freedom.

I walked out onto the great ranch-style porch of the lodge and felt quite small as I looked out over the mountains cascaded with fall's rich tapestry. I pondered what I'd just seen.

Time had not healed these wounds.

Secrecy had not made them any less painful.

A simple, tearstained confession had helped these women move toward ending the imprisonment and the beginning of healing.

———————— ⊰•⊱ ————————

Some snake skeletons have little legs on them, as though the snake used to have legs. That may puzzle scientists who believe in evolution, but it does not surprise me. I am tickled with delight. God told us right in His Word that He removed the snake's legs because of how it had been used of Satan. The snake's consequences were the loss of his legs.

Know this. God is just and does not omit the consequences of our sin . . . like those skeletons prove.

Making poor sexual choices will bring consequences. I am not talking about pregnancy or AIDS or STDs. I am talking about the cancer that eats away at the heart.

God does forgive. As I told you in chapter 4, that forgiveness is immediate. But being forgiven is not the same as being restored or healed. Eve had to accept the consequences of her sin, which were to experience pain in childbirth and to have an unquenchable desire for her husband who would rule over or "be in charge of" her.

The very saddest consequence of sexual sin that I have seen is that the day does come when someone you know and love will need to hear your confession. For me that day came after five years of marriage.

It had been ten years since I had "robbed" my marriage bed. During that decade, I had struggled with my self-image, my value in Christ, my sense of integrity. I had determined to tell Bob about my sin before he proposed to me, or at least before I answered his proposal. Then, he surprised me and proposed to me onstage in front of two thousand people in a more romantic way than I could have dreamed up myself. To say the least, it was a bad time to bring up my hidden past. Our engagement was filled with moments when I tried to tell him. And the first several months of marriage, I tried again. This hidden sin was robbing me of many moments of joy. I read book after book searching for permission to never tell him. Eventually, I kind of stuck the notion that anybody needed to know in a drawer, like you might a piece of junk.

Then one day, I was driving down the road with my brand-new baby girl in the seat behind me as I listened to Dr. James Dobson interview a woman concerning raising sexually pure daughters. I only heard two sentences.

Dr. Dobson: What is the number one question teenage girls ask their moms?

The Woman: Mom, did you wait?

My heart broke into millions of pieces at that moment. One day my Lexi would ask me that question.

That night, I sat for three hours in a dark bedroom with my husband until a tearstained confession could make its way out of my lips. At that exact moment and in my husband's tender arms, I felt release. I felt healing. I felt free.

During all those years of hiding, I had been like Adam and Eve in the garden sewing together fig leaves. How pathetic! Those leaves may have camouflaged their shame, but I doubt they made them feel comfy and cozy. When God came to them and made them own up to their actions . . . *then,* the great God of the universe clothed them in garments of skin. If He had not done so, they might have spent the rest of their lives finding fresh fig leaves to replace the wilted ones!

If you think that no one needs to know about your sin, you are believing a great lie of Satan.

I never understood this completely until this summer when I was at a con-

*Josh McDowell
on Sexual Healing*

Dannah: *How important
do you think confession
is to the process of
sexual healing?*

Josh: *I think it is very critical.
I am not sure a girl can
truly experience God's
forgiveness apart from
her parents. She can't.
God wants to express
verbally—through Mom,
Dad, an older sister,
a pastor's wife, or
someone like that—
that He forgives them.*

ference. As the leader read, "Confess your sins to each other and pray for each other so that you may be healed" from James 5:16, it all came together in my mind. God's forgiveness was immediate. The healing was something that would come more slowly and through the nurturing of other Christians as they verbalized to me God's loving forgiveness.

Oddly enough, as I slowly began to confess within the confines of close-knit Bible study groups and small gatherings of women, I found that many of them were also hiding in silence and fear from mistakes in their past. In my confession, they found the courage to confess and begin the process of healing too.

In other words, speaking about it frees you and others too! Don't let Satan's knowledge of what you have done blackmail you into silence.

I am not saying the whole world needs to know or that you have to write a book about it. (Can you believe God asked me to do this?) But find one person who is older and wiser and who is making right choices in her life and confess. After your confession to God, the most important people for any confession are the ones most directly affected. Your mom would be my first suggestion, but if that seems impossible to you right now, choose someone else to whom to confess and from whom to borrow courage and advice to someday go to your mom. Use great discretion in choosing someone and ask God for guidance, but don't waste any more years or months hiding.

CHAPTER SIXTEEN

7 secret

PURITY
WATCHES
BURNING
FLAMES

finding

m.o.r.e.

to help

you

7
secret

PURITY WATCHES
BURNING FLAMES

Finding M.O.R.E. to Help You

Your path led through the sea, your way through the mighty waters, though your footprints were not seen.
(PSALM 77:19)

"I need to be held," I confided in my husband.

"Then you come right here," he said, plopping himself on the sofa. He wrapped his arms around me, engulfing me in his scent and his warmth. This was a safe place. I felt warm tears flowing down my cheeks as I relaxed into his embrace.

"You can think you are really good and that you have really tried to live a godly life," I stammered through my pain. "Then, you look back and realize you're not at all worth the chances you have been given."

Through the silence that followed, our hearts spoke. He knew my secret pain. Last night was the night we had planned together for many, many months. My heart's desire was, is, and always will be to live a lifestyle of purity, but in high school I detoured from that pursuit long enough to get tangled up by Lust. Like no other sin, moments of unbridled passion had intertwined my life painfully into another's. I had to make one final call to cut the last fraying cord. After fifteen years, I had called Michael to request forgiveness and to offer mine. It was a final act to sever the past, but it did not come without discomfort. Any moment of passion that was lustfully lived out in that youthful relationship was not equal to the pain that I felt searing my heart at this moment.

"Who am I to write this book?" I cried.

"Dannah," he said as he cradled my head in his hands. "Who else has this passion? Who else understands the pain? Who else is talking about the glory? Who else?"

"But . . ." I resisted.

"I was always held to a higher standard by you than by any other girl I ever dated. You were strong, uncompromised, and pure," he affirmed. "That's all I know of you. That's all that matters to me."

"But . . ." He pressed his hand to my lips.

I had worked for years to aggressively live a lifestyle of purity, but at this moment I felt the demons of lust and pride taunting me with memories they'd created just for me. I felt as if they'd brought legions of their cruel friends to surround my home.

But angels were fighting equally hard and were about to set the stage to win a battle in my life.

The telephone broke the silence. It was Meghan. She is one of "my girls." I met her on one of my retreats, and we are working together to build purity and contentment and wholeness into her life. It is not an easy battle. Bulimia and anorexia pursue her. A broken heart from a past relationship provides enough pain to bring frequent tears. I hadn't heard from her in weeks and was beginning to feel she might not need me for much more of her journey. Her call confirmed that she did.

"I have sooo much to tell you," she said. "I am doing great, but I really need to talk."

"How's Thursday?" I asked.

"It's a date," she said.

I crawled into bed with the knowledge that God was using me in spite of who I am, not because of who I am. This ministry is not about me. It is all about Him. Little did I know that in the morning following this dark hour, He would lovingly pour out His Spirit to affirm my usefulness, His omnipresent leadership, and your final secret.

That was last night. I am actually in the middle of writing this book, but I know without a doubt that God wrote this chapter in my heart this morning. I confessed my sin again and admitted my feeling of inferiority. I thanked Him for Meghan's call to encourage me and opened my Bible to read my psalm for today. And there at the end of Psalm 77, verse 19's great truth was revealed to me like only God can do.

"*Your* [God's] path led through the sea, *your* way through the mighty waters . . ." (italics added).

The psalmist was writing of the Israelites' walk through the Red Sea, which was parted when Moses raised his hands. They were leaving a land of slavery to find God's Promised Land. The psalmist acknowledged God as the One who actually parted the seas even though it was through Moses' upraised hands. But then, he wrote, "Though your footprints were not seen . . ."

They missed God's footprints! They stomped right across them and never saw them! Oh, how sad. God allowed His own majestic footprints to be stomped out as clumsy Israelites made their way across the sandy water bed, craning their necks to look to make sure old Moses still had his hands raised high in the sky. God lovingly gave them Moses' living hands because He knew that was what they needed to walk in His footprints.

When I think of Moses, I think of the burning bush and the passion that it brought to his life. He took some of the power of God that he received at that bush and used it in the lives of other people. When I think of women in my life who were like Moses to me, I think of a burning, passionate flame.

I thought of the women through the years who have encouraged me and led me out of barren lands . . . sinful lands . . . boring lands . . . hopeless lands . . . old lands. Some offered words of encouragement. Some chastened me. Some forced me out. But always at pivotal points in my life, there has been a "Moses" to be my burning flame. I thought about the times when I was stuck or when I entered into a bad land and noticed the lack of anyone significant influencing my

How Old? How Wise?

A Washington, D.C., based Best Friends program encourages fifth through ninth grade students to encourage each other to remain abstinent. It's working! In a 1990 follow-up survey, none of the Best Friends girls were sexually active as compared to 37 percent of a control group.[1] Remember, these girls were no older than ninth grade but were making a great impact on one another. One of the greatest mentors I know is a senior in high school named Lauren Webb. It seems every time I turn around I hear another girl in our youth group saying, "Well, Lauren told me to . . ." They take her advice and they let her hold them accountable. She is a great burning flame. Older and wiser can be a matter of a few short years. Just make sure she is making right choices in her life. This isn't about having another friend. It's about having a leader.

life. I noticed isolation prior to my bad choices to live stuck in a place where God did not want me to be. I reached for my journal and wrote a silly little poem about my burning flames and how I needed them.

I sat pondering Moses' role as a burning flame. Then, God gave me MORE! I reached for my *Experiencing God: Youth Edition,* which our youth group is studying right now. Guess who week 2, lesson 2 is all about? Moses. (Isn't God's timing wonderful!) It starts out, "Who delivered the children of Israel from Egypt? Moses or God? God did. God chose to bring Moses into a relationship with Himself so that He—God—could deliver Israel."[2] Wow!

It wasn't about Moses.
It was all about God.

This book isn't about me.
It is all about God.

Oh, I hope that you have begun or continued a journey toward God's promised land of a fantastic sexual union. There is probably one man who is waiting to be one with you, just as you wait to be one with him. I hope that I have been a burning flame in your life to give you the passion to follow the majestic footprints of God.

But soon you will close the pages of this book and will no longer see my burning passion.

Find a burning flame.

Don't do it tomorrow or next week. Ask God for guidance right now and find a burning flame in your life to look to for guidance and encouragement.

She should be M.O.R.E.
. . . Making right choices (living righteously) in her current life
. . . Older and wiser
. . . Readily accessible so she can watch you and you can watch her
. . . Excited to burn for you

Write Your Story

Grab your journal and write down a few names of people who have burned brightly for you in the past. Jot down the names of some women that you know who are M.O.R.E. Choose one of them to approach. Write your request to God to put it on her heart to burn for you!

it's your
turn

Find a burning flame, my friend.

And promise me that when someone else finds you . . .

   . . . no matter how old you are

   . . . no matter what clutter lies in your past

   . . . no matter how busy you are

   . . . no matter how inferior you may feel . . .

you

will

be a

burning flame

for her.

NOTES

1. Kristine Napier, *The Power of Abstinence* (New York: Avon Books, 1996), 89–90.

2. Henry T. Blackaby and Claude V. King, *Experiencing God: Youth Edition* (Nashville: Lifeway Press, 1994), 27.

CHAPTER SEVENTEEN

THE
PAYMENTS
ON THE
PEARL
CONTINUE

using the

seven

secrets

after your

wedding

day

THE PAYMENTS ON THE PEARL CONTINUE

Using the Seven Secrets After Your Wedding Day

> *Though one may be overpowered, two can defend themselves. A cord of three strands is not quickly broken.*
> (ECCLESIASTES 4:12)

Don't close this book and say, "What a rosy little life Dannah lives." There have been some really neat and romantic memories created in the first ten years of my marriage, but it hasn't been perfect. No marriage is without pain. Bob and I have made each other cry a lot. We've struggled to continue the pursuit of purity in both of our lives, and sometimes we have failed. Once, the only thing holding us together was Jesus. I remember writing in my journal, "My cord is severed. Bob's cord is severed. Lord, You are the only cord in our 'cord of three strands' holding fast." (I think God liked that admission. He soon tied those severed spots into nice tight knots!)

Marriage is not easy. In fact, I am very thankful for the seven secrets that God gave me during my dating years. I still use them a great deal.

I STILL NEED TO REMEMBER THAT *purity is a process,* because I still mess up and have to get back on track.

I STILL NEED TO REMEMBER THAT *purity dreams of its future,* because it keeps my marriage fresh. (I have this really wild dream of a huger-than-my-wedding celebration for one of our special anniversaries . . . when we can afford it. Dreaming of that day keeps me falling in love with Bob. And silly as it may seem, I dream of us sitting on a porch in rocking chairs with great-grandchildren crawling into our laps.)

I STILL NEED TO REMEMBER THAT *purity is governed by its value* or I might buy things at the store that I should not wear and I might forget to behave becomingly in front of my husband. (It is important to maintain some mystique!)

I STILL NEED TO REMEMBER THAT *purity speaks boldly* so that I can keep Bob on track spiritually. He does the same for me.

I STILL NEED TO REMEMBER THAT *purity watches burning flames*. I stick very close to my mom, Kay Barker, who is my favorite burning flame. Women like my friend Tippy Duncan have helped me to be faithful and make right choices in my marriage. I expose myself daily to burning flames who don't even know me, like author Becky Tirabassi, who convinced me that prayer could change my life. (It did.) I listen to Twila Paris every single day because her music teaches me to worship at the very throne of God. I've learned that not following the lead of burning flames is detrimental. So, I pursue them aggressively.

I STILL NEED TO REMEMBER THAT *purity embraces wise guidance* because I am still learning who I am through my family and how that fits into who Bob is because of his.

BUT MOST OF ALL, I NEED TO ALWAYS REMIND MYSELF THAT *purity loves its Creator at any cost*. Now that I am in a covenant relationship with one man, my faithfulness to him is a portrait of my faithfulness to my Creator.

---·⟨⟩·---

I am sitting in a condo one hour away from home right now. I have come to finish this book. I don't mind saying that it is also a nice break from seemingly insurmountable obligations that Bob and I are finding ourselves under right now. The past few weeks have been filled with tension as we seek to make it through some tight deadlines. Last night I spent an hour on the telephone "debating" with Bob whose fault it is . . . his or mine. We ended the conversation with prayer, but we both felt angry and agitated when it was over. This morning I went to God to tell Him how terribly selfish my husband is being. (Ha!) I was brutally honest. "God, I am very angry at him. How can I fellowship with You when I am so sure he is wrong?" Then I opened up my Rebecca St. James's *You're the Voice* devotional, which I am going through with Lauren, one of the girls I mentor. My lesson today was entitled "You Then Me." It was about selfishness. I felt convicted. I was the one being selfish, so I called Bob to apologize. Somehow, our conversation turned into another irreconcilable debate.

I cried. There seemed to be no way to work it out.

"Maybe we should just hang up," I suggested as calmly as I could after a good fifteen minutes of getting nowhere fast. "I am only becoming more upset, and I really need to focus. I can't focus when we are not united."

There was a long pause.

"Dannah, I don't want to fight. We are united," Bob answered. "We both love the Lord, and we are equally committed to loving each other. Let's just forget the whole first half of this conversation. We will work this out."

And we did. Very quickly too.

Why? Because Jesus is the very center of our love life.

He was before we even knew each other.

He was when we were dating.

He always will be.

Our love for each other is merely a portrait of our faithful love for our Creator . . . the Pearl of Great Price.

Recently Bob slipped this note into my suitcase as I left to conduct a purity retreat.

> *Sweetheart:*
> *You are my pearl of great price. I cherish every moment*
> *with you. I cannot wait until tomorrow to spend the whole*
> *weekend with you.*
> > *I love you,*
> > *B*

———— ❧⋅❧ ————

May our marriage and yours-to-come
be a portrait of your devotion for the Pearl of Great Price.
He costs everything.
He is worth the price.

appendix

INTERVIEWS FROM THE HEART

Five Christian Celebrities Talk About Love, Sex, and Dating

These wonderful Christian celebrities took time to share intimate thoughts about themselves with you and me. I used short excerpts from each of them in the book. They were so good, I wanted you to hear more of what they said for you.

Steven Curtis Chapman

SINGER/SONGWRITER

I met Steven Curtis Chapman on his great big beautiful bus. (His boys were bouncing around in the front watching Bullwinkle cartoons.) My focus with him was on his relationship with his teenage daughter, Emily. Like you, her relationship with her dad is vital to her development of healthy relationships with other guys. Let's take a peek at how Steven Curtis Chapman does the "dad thing."

Dannah: Tell me about your daughter, Emily.

SCC: When I talk about my family, I try to be real honest. When I say Emily is *the* coolest thirteen-year-old, I am not saying it because I am her dad. My wife and I constantly say she is who she is in spite of us, not because of us. She has a heart for missions. With her Christmas money, she bought a book on international adoption. She is putting some serious heat on her mom and I to adopt a baby from another country. That gives you a little idea of what kind of a girl Emily is.

Dannah: What is your favorite thing to do together?

SCC: It's hard to pick out specific things. We just like hangin' out. One of my favorite things is tucking her into bed. I just go up and pray with her. Some of the coolest conversations happen at night. Her brothers aren't around driving everyone crazy and she will start to talk.

I love taking her to basketball practice. She has to be there at like 6:30 A.M. Sometimes we don't say anything. Then, other times we really talk.

Dannah: There are so many statistics which say that girls pursue sex when they don't get affection from their dads. But often at the age of eleven, twelve, thirteen, they begin to individuate and need a little space. Some girls I work with look at dads like you and say, "I wish I had a dad like that." They don't realize that some of this individuation is something that they bring on. And that it hurts the dads. I cannot really influence the dads, but I wonder if as you look at your daughter's life is there something that you see her doing . . . choices she makes, things that she does . . . to build into the relationship?

SCC: Emily has never been a real touchy, feeling kind of girl. That was hard for us at first. Even when she was born, she just wanted to be in her crib. Right off the bat, I wondered how was I going to give her the affection she needs without her feeling smothered. My challenge has been to let her pick her moments. We'll be at a Little League ball game; I will all of a sudden realize she is just hanging on me. She is the one movin' towards me. Then, I try to take as much advantage of that as I can. I see that as one thing she does.

And I think I see her trusting us. She believes us when we say, "Emily, whatever you think, whatever you feel . . . we have been there." It is a leap of faith for a girl to trust her mom, but especially her dad . . . to let them on the inside loop of what was going on.

I remember one night she came home and we could just see something in her eyes. Pretty soon, she just fell apart and opened up and told us everything. She said, "Are you all mad at me?" That she would even entrust us with that information! We all started bawling then. We said, "No, Emily, we just are so proud of you." (Thank You, Lord!) She trusts us. She chooses to trust us.

Dannah: This last question is just about you. You have lived a godly example for so many people, but no matter who you are, there will always be temptation. You have made choices to live a lifestyle of purity. What would be one moment that you could say, "I chose a path of purity in my life and I am proud of that"?

SCC: Well, our life is made up of a lot of those moments. Hmmm? I am hesitant only because I think, "How honest do I want to be?" There was a relationship that I was in long ago. I was out on my own, all alone for the first time. There was a girl that I was dating. It was not a really deep relationship. We were kissing and had kind of gotten involved. But I had always known that I was saving myself. I wanted my wedding night to be the first night I was that intimate and it would be with the woman I married. But I knew that in this relationship if I wanted to go down that route, she was willing. It was like a bucket of water in my face. It was not even an option. I cannot say it is a moment that I was proud of, as much as it was a moment that God had really trained me for. For a brief moment, I was caught up in the motion. I was a nineteen-year-old young man and a light came on and I said, "Think about all the implications, physically, emotionally, and spiritually." That was the beginning of the end of that relationship. God had built a real strong foundation in me. I am thankful that sex is and was an amazing thing on my wedding night because I saved myself for that night. I am so thankful for people along the way to help me build that foundation.

Dannah's suggested SCC resource:

Steven Curtis Chapman's Greatest Hits

You'll hear some of his best stuff on this CD. Listen closely to the words in "For the Sake of the Call," and then listen to "The Great Adventure." Hear how the price of following Christ is worth it.

Josh McDowell

CAMPUS CRUSADE FOR CHRIST

Josh McDowell agreed to meet me at a very loud and crowded Burger King during one of the Extreme conferences in 1999. Wearing his Hilfiger sweat suit and sipping a Pepsi, he gave a touch of his wealth of knowledge on the subject of sex. He offers some good advice on how we can encourage and protect one another.

Dannah: A lot of young women who have sinned sexually seem to be locked in this position of blackmail that Satan puts them in.

Josh: No girl can experience true forgiveness without the body of Christ. We've got to commit to control our tongues so confession can take place.

Dannah: So many of the girls I meet think that purity is a fixed point. The problem is that some girls who are technically virgins are living very impure lifestyles, but they consider themselves pure. Then, there are some girls who are trying to start over, but they feel so impure. What would you say to them?

Josh: In Romans 8 Paul talks about walking in the Spirit. It is not either/or. Paul says if you are led of the Spirit . . . if you are walking with the Spirit. It doesn't mean that there are no times of carnality. The overall description of your life is one of spirituality. It does not mean there are not spurts of carnality. That's why [John] gives us, "If we are faithful to confess our sins, he is faithful and just and will forgive us our sins." But over all, there is a spirituality to you. Living a life of purity doesn't mean [one has never had] spurts of impurity. But a life of purity is that when there is impurity, it is handled in the biblical way. It is confessed. That's a pure life. It is not either/or.

Dannah: So, where would you encourage girls to draw "the line" as far as physical contact?

Josh: This society thinks that if there isn't vaginal penetration, there isn't sex. In 1 Thessalonians 4 . . . it says, "This is the will of God that you abstain from sexual immorality. Learn to possess your body, not like the Gentiles who cannot control their bodies." *Anything* you do that will cause the one you are with to *desire* to go all the way . . . it is impurity. Sometimes holding hands is too much. If you spend time with a girl who comes from a broken home, just holding her hand can trigger a desire to go all the way. You take someone with a loving father, a happy mother and father, holding hands, kissing doesn't trigger those things. . . . Even jokes, conversation, can cause a person to desire to go all the way. So, I teach my kids to play it conservatively.

Dannah: What's the best reason to live a lifestyle of purity?

Josh: There is not one place in the Bible that calls sex sinful. Period. Not one single verse. There are many verses that say the misuse of sex is sinful, but there is not one verse that says that sex is sinful. Scripture is full of wonderful descriptions of sex. Proverbs 5:19 says, "Rejoice always in her breasts. Let her breasts satisfy you always and be captivated by her." Do you take the Bible literally? I sure like to here! Let her breasts satisfy you at all times. The Hebrew word for *captivate* means "intoxicate always." What it says is, let her breasts satisfy you at all times and be intoxicated by her sex.

Sex is so beautiful, *it is worth protecting*.

Dannah's pick of Josh McDowell's resource:
The Love Killer

This novelplus, as it is called, is a story laced with great truths. It answers the question, "What is the secret of making your love last?"

Rebecca St. James

SINGER/SONGWRITER

The third time is the charm. I finally got to interview Rebecca on my third attempt. First I drove to Gatlinburg, but a blizzard delayed me and I missed the interview. Then, we were scheduled to speak the same day she performed for the pope's visit to St. Louis, but I was flying out of St. Louis and the security was extra tight because of the pope so things didn't work out. Finally, my phone rang at home. "Hello, this is Rebecca!" She called. After praying over me, she invited you and me into her private hopes and dreams in regards to her future husband.

Dannah: Do you have a vision of the man you will marry? A goal? A dream?

Rebecca: Well, yeah, I definitely have a vision of a little bit of what he will be like. I just kind of picture him just having this consuming love for God that is just so beautiful and so challenging to me. That leads me and challenges me. I definitely want him to be a spiritual leader to me. I think that because I know that he is going to be a man after God's own heart and purity is going to be important to him too. He is going to be waiting for me. That helps comfort me in the waiting process.

Dannah: Is it hard for you? Do you struggle?

Rebecca: I definitely have. I struggle with loneliness . . . especially in my early teens. I just moved from Australia . . . the other side of the world. I didn't know anyone here. I didn't have any friends. I was homeschooling. The only time I got to be with friends was when I was at youth group or church. And the people there already had their friends. They didn't need me. In what I am called to do now . . . the ministry that God has given me . . . you can be amongst people and still be lonely or want that companionship of someone who really understands you. That loneliness turns me to God. He is the only friend that truly understands and that is truly there all the time. I cannot be living in another season of my life. I can look forward to the future, but I cannot be living *for* that time. I have got to be living here and now for God and giving Him my all. And not wishing I was with someone else.

Dannah: If you had to select one thing and say this has been my greatest blessing in living a lifestyle of purity, this is the one blessing that I can already see, what would you choose?

Rebecca: I think just there's something very beautiful about purity. I think of Mother Teresa. She had such a purity and a beauty about her even though she wasn't stunning to look at. One of the things that God has really put on my heart is that He has encouraged me to be beautiful inside and in my heart. There is just a feeling of "I am saving myself for that person and I can grow in beauty for him."

One of the things I talk about in concert is that if people have made the mistake of having sex outside of marriage that they can become a "recycled" virgin. There is a second chance. They can have that purity restored in God's sight. God forgives us and purifies us and makes us whole again. I have had a great response to that. More than any other message, people have really responded to the message of purity.

Dannah's pick of Rebecca's resources:

You're the Voice: 40 More Days with God

This great devotional will help you to get into the practice of being consistent if you are struggling with your prayer life. If you already have a great prayer life, it's deep enough to challenge you too.

Joshua Harris

AUTHOR OF I KISSED DATING GOODBYE

Joshua is married! (And he did that without dating!) I caught up to him at home one evening while he was nursing his new wife, Shannon, back to health from the flu. In this interview, he offers us a special insight into the romance of being single.

Dannah: When you set your standard to "kiss dating good-bye," did that automatically erase any desires or tugging at the heart? Or did you still feel the cost?

Joshua: Oh definitely. The hardest part in waiting on God's timing and choosing to submit that area of your life to Him is trusting Him that He really has your good in mind. In the area of relationships the battle is always, "Should I leave this in God's hands or should I take that into my own hands?" I think that is even a bigger struggle for the girls. They start thinking, *If I don't start making something happen, if I don't start to manipulate. . . .* The terrible thing about that is it does sometimes get the guy. You might get what you are wanting in the short term, but never what you want in the long term. Because you got a guy's attention, but for the wrong reasons. Or you pursue something at the wrong time in your life and even though it is good for a while, in the long run you see that it has distracted you from doing what you were really supposed to be doing.

Dannah: Some young women I meet think the cost is too high. They think that not dating or waiting on God is just too hard. What would you say to them?

Joshua: It has got to be something that comes from their heart or it is just a bunch of rules. I would ask them a few questions. What is it that is motivating you to pursue this relationship? What's your purpose? If you don't have a relationship with God, if that is not an all-consuming relationship with Him, if that is not your driving motivation—you are not going to have the ability to do it. It seems burdensome and hard. The people I know who are not pursuing romance are not doing it out of a "Whoa-is-me-I-am-such-a-martyr" attitude. It is a joyful thing when the motivation is God's best. When you do it for that reason, it is not a hard thing.

The things the world has to offer—short-term romance, dates on Fridays—can be exciting and pleasing for a while. You have to look at the long-term too. It's not just the moment. Is the outcome of the way you are living really bringing you the joy and satisfaction that you want?

A lot of us have forgotten how romantic the waiting is. I think singleness and not being attached to someone can be a very romantic thing. You are not just waiting for the sake of waiting . . . you are waiting for *that* person.

Dannah: What is the most wonderful gift God has given back to you as a result of your choosing to live a lifestyle of purity?

Joshua: There is such freedom in it. It is not a "holier-than-thou" attitude, because when I think of God's standards, I don't think of myself as pure or holy. But in pursuing a lifestyle of purity there is so much freedom. The thing I see in the times in my life when I didn't do that, is that slavery lies in the sin. People who don't pursue purity sometimes think they want to be free. What they don't see is how impurity enslaves you. It takes this wonderful gift of intimacy and it dirties it. It makes you its slave as you serve your lustful desires. Living a life of purity just gives you so much freedom. I got married five months ago. That was the first time to enjoy the gift of sexual intimacy with my wife. There was such freedom in that. Freedom from guilt. Freedom from regret. Pursuing purity brings freedom.

Dannah's recommendation of Joshua's book:
I Kissed Dating Goodbye
If you are tired of the dating game, kiss dating good-bye. Joshua offers you the secrets to enjoy true purity and a purposeful singleness.

Becky Tirabassi

AUTHOR OF LET PRAYER CHANGE YOUR LIFE

Becky Tirabassi is one of the reasons I have written this book. Her call to pray for one hour a day changed my life. I began to really hear God's voice in a new and dynamic way. I pursued her for an interview for several months and finally got a few minutes with her just before she took off to catch a plane for a speaking engagement. She has got some good thoughts for you.

Dannah: How significant has confession to others been in your healing process?

Becky: Well, I think when you expose the truth about yourself and the truth about your past, it doesn't have the power to be a lie anymore. The embarrassment or the shame, once you confess it, is gone. You begin to see yourself as a new person, and the Enemy cannot use it against you. James 5:16 says, "Confess your sins one to another so that you may be healed." Confession . . . it's *the* place of your healing. Rather than even just being forgiven, you find healing there. It is almost like tithing; you don't know what you're gonna get or how you're gonna get it. So, you just step forward. There *is* something on the other side that releases your shame and brings healing.

Dannah: What advice could you give to girls whose mothers are not open and comfortable in talking about sexual issues?

Becky: Not every mother and daughter are going to have great communication. In those cases, you will probably find that your youth worker or another significant godly woman can be influential. But what I would really encourage . . . you need to be in the Word of God. You need to ask God for direction. You can go your whole life looking for direction from a man, a husband, somebody. But you need to look at all that through the Word, especially if your mom's not even a Christian or your dad's not a Christian. The Word of God should be in your life daily to evaluate any input you receive.

Dannah's pick of Becky Tirabassi's resources:
Quiet Times Student Prayer Journal
and Let Prayer Change Your Life
You need an organized, systematic way to pray. *Quiet Times Student Prayer Journal* is specifically for busy students who desire a practical, organized prayer life. If you really want to get excited about prayer, pick up a copy of *Let Prayer Change Your Life* to go along with that *Journal*.

appendix B

LETTERS FROM THE HEART

Four Burning Flames Tell Their Stories and Their Secrets

A Special Letter on Sexual Abuse

Dear Young Woman:

I wanted to write to you to tell you how much I admire your commitment to sexual purity. Sometimes the quest for sexual purity is met with great resistance. Pushing past this resistance will be a true test of your character. In some unique cases, it may be met with a resistance so strong and unnatural that it seems nearly impossible to live a lifestyle of purity. I know. I felt a strong, unnatural resistance in my quest for purity. I came to find out that it was more than simply fighting my flesh. There was something very unpleasant lurking in my past.

I was very young when I was sexually molested by my father's friend from work. My parents had trusted him to baby-sit while they went to a work-related function. I was terrified when the covers were thrown off me and he touched me in ways I had never been touched before. I tried to forget the event, but the damage was permanent. Strong sexual feelings were associated with fear, secrecy, shame, and perversion. I felt powerless and betrayed. This led to much confusion about my sexuality. I acted out this confusion with no hope of purity. After many years of self-destructive promiscuous behavior, which included abusive relationships, I met the husband God had planned for me. It was in the early years of our marriage that the sexual damage was evident. Fear and infertility ruled our intimacy.

But hope was around the corner. I met Jesus Christ and surrendered my life to Him. That brought the first step of healing. I could not have even begun to heal without Jesus as my Savior.

There is a verse in Song of Solomon that states, "Do not arouse or awaken love until it so desires." When I read that verse it spoke to me about the sin of one man damaging what God had planned to be a holy and pure act in marriage. I was awoken and then aroused, but it was not what I desired. What God had planned to be aroused by my loving husband had already been awoken. It was the touch of God in my life that healed the sinful touches of the past. I know now that many young women who are acting out sexually are as confused as I was. I understand the struggle to feel in control of your sexual feelings. God is with you. He will never hurt you. Surrendering to His ways only brings peace, joy, and wholeness.

There is often a period of total denial and mysterious uncertainty that precedes the acceptance of sexual abuse. Are you unable to combat the temptations placed before you? Do you feel your sexual desires overpowering your will? Does your mind reject the truth that attaining purity after sexual defilement is possible? Or . . . at the total other end of the spectrum . . . do you tend to avoid the subject of sexuality? Are you unable to accept God's gift of sexuality to you? Is the idea of pure and holy sex repulsive to you? You are more likely to answer yes to these questions if you have had sexual abuse in your past.

The extent of spiritual and emotional damage following sexual abuse is difficult to recognize. Broken women tend to minimize what happened to them. If you are aware of sexual abuse in your past, believe this: God wants you to bring it to Him. It is not too dark for Him. He will bring everything into the light and heal the damage inflicted on your soul. Under the shadow of His wings there is safety. He longs for you to come into His arms to cry out the deep hidden pain. He cares about stolen purity.

Find a godly woman who will intercede for you, preferably your mother. Private sexual shame heals when publicly grieved. Your public may be the small group you are now in. Small, confidential groups of women are one of the tools God uses to heal those once sexually abused. A professional Christian counselor can guide you in the healing process and maintain your confidentiality. But don't try to do it alone. It won't work.

Let me give you a little assignment that you may find very emotionally freeing. Read the Song of Solomon. This is God's description of the relationship of a husband and wife. Let the words of this book be your prayer for a loving, intimate relationship. Begin to see yourself as a virgin bride waiting for the man God has planned for you. Do not accept the lie that God will not totally accept you because you have been defiled. Fight the battle in your mind to see yourself as damaged goods.

God has a great plan for you, His precious daughter. You may have been robbed of innocence as a child, but you can still be pure and restored to wholeness by the work of His hand. Never give up hope for your commitment to purity. He will make all things beautiful in His time.

Under His Wings,
Linda Cochrane

Linda is the Executive Director of Hopeline Women's Center in Connecticut. She is the author of *Forgiven and Set Free* and coauthor of *Healing a Father's Heart*. Both are postabortion Bible studies. She is coauthor of *A Time to Heal*, a Bible study for healing traumatic experiences. Soon to be released is *Standing Pure*, a Bible study she has written specifically for restoring broken sexuality.

A Special Letter on Waiting for God's Timing

Dear Friend,

I call you "friend" because I am sharing with you from my heart. How I wish I could be sitting down with you at some fun restaurant somewhere, or maybe talking with you while walking on the beach. I'd love to talk *with you* about this story, for I am sure you have a story to tell as well.

I'm a pleaser . . . I want so badly for others to be pleased with me—my friends, family. I've always been that way. Can you identify with that?

It was extremely difficult—no matter how confident I seemed on the outside— to keep wanting to make the right decisions. I had so much love to give, and I wanted to express this love somehow. I wanted this man of my dreams one day to be pleased—very pleased—with his choice of me, his wife. But so many times "my husband"—whoever he was—seemed so far away. I knew the "shouldn'ts"—but I didn't realize that God wanted to show me *how and where to focus my love and energy* for the people I cared so much about.

There was such a strong desire within me to please—how could I be faithful to my decision to live a lifestyle of purity? I went through high school, college, and several years as a single working woman. I had a few pretty serious relationships in there, but they never seemed to be just right. I faced many doubts. Relationships never seemed to work out or meet my expectations. I was beginning to wonder if I should give up.

I felt sometimes I was all by myself in this struggle, which was huge to me. "Could anyone else really understand?" Everyone I knew had a boyfriend, was engaged, or was talking about "this perfect guy they had just met". . . and were asking me *where was mine?* Where *was* mine? I started to doubt, and I felt like there wasn't much encouragement where I was in my life at that time.

My understanding changed when I began to see this was much more than a decision about my body . . . it was a decision about my heart! God used several strong Christian friends in powerful ways in my life right when I needed them. They pushed me to really hold on tight to God and to the promises He had for my life.

"'For I know the plans I have for you,' declares the Lord, 'plans to prosper you and not to harm you, plans to give you hope and a future. . . . You will seek me and find me when you seek me with all your heart. I will be found by you,' declares the Lord" (Jeremiah 29:11, 13-14).

I realized my first and most important person to please was the One who loved me the most. The One who had sacrificed so much so that I could live—*my Father God!* How I needed to please Him! (1 Corinthians 6:19–20).

During what seemed to be a long time of "just me and God," I really grew closer to Him. I began to be much more confident—He really *did* have an awesome plan for my life. My struggle became an opportunity to hold on to something strongly *because of who I was holding on for!*

I was focused on God, waiting in Him. My desire truly was for *Him*—and suddenly someone noticed! At the age of 26, I met Tim Powers.

Tim Powers seemed to be everything I had ever desired! As I began to get to know him, I could tell he respected girls and himself and had a strong relationship with God. But would he really understand my heart—respect me for my stand? It had not been easy, and not everyone really understood. *(It was a hard but true realization that not all Christian guys take a stand for purity.)*

We began those long conversations of getting to know each other. I was learning more about his character—what was really important to him. I was very excited to hear he had also taken a stand for purity with his life and was saving his body for his wife . . . even at the age of 34! That's how much he valued her! He was choosing her over anyone else, wanting to give his whole person as a gift to her—not once, but for the rest of his life! Wow! Was this possible? Such an awesome guy was waiting to give himself totally to someone he had never met?! (I could tell by these thoughts, I had believed the lie that "there couldn't be a guy out there who could take this stand." *Especially not one who would be "my type of guy" . . . who I'd want to marry for life.)*

Well, God blew me away! Tim was beyond my expectations! *(God loves to do that—give to us beyond our every dream!)* In a horse-drawn carriage on New Year's Eve, Tim asked me to be his wife. Our wedding day and marriage have been the greatest gifts I have ever received.

Looking back, I realize even more the value of the precious gifts of trust, pure love, and commitment given to me. We have given each other an exclusive gift—the sole right of treasuring each other's bodies. There is no substitute for that gift! There has been such trust between us. We know our heart values given by God and continued focus on Him will keep us strong!

God's best for me has been this man who loves God and who honored and respected his body and mine before he even knew me. I know this has to be of the Lord . . . and to Him I am so very grateful! (2 Corinthians 3:4 –5).

You, my friend, are God's very special treasure—He values your life no matter what decisions you have made. Pray for a man whose godly heart you can reflect. What a privilege this will be for you! Trust Him for the hope of all He has to give you. He has only His most precious gifts to give His children. Trust Him and commit to stand for His best—*wait on God!* He'll give you the strength and courage you need. He is the giver of every good and perfect gift!

"Delight yourself in the Lord and he will give you the desires of your heart" (Psalm 37:4). *(A promise from God . . . who never breaks His promises!)*

With much love and hope!
Kimberly Powers

P.S. Please write and tell me your story. . . . I'd love to hear from you!

Kimberly and Tim Powers are the founders of Walk The Talk Youth Ministries, Inc., which offers two outstanding youth conferences. Ground Zero is a coed junior and senior high conference focusing on having a radical and even warlike mentality to fight the Enemy. In Search of a Princess is a junior high girls' conference that uses the story of Esther to build self-esteem in young women. E-mail: Kimberly@WTTYM.ORG

———————— ⟨3·⟩ ————————

A Special Letter on Singleness

Dear Friend,

I've read a lot of books that called single women "old maids" or "spinsters," which makes singleness sound like a bad thing. I am single, 32 years old, so I guess I could be considered an old maid. (Hey, maybe I'm even a spinster.) I am a virgin, and I've never been kissed. I get tired of questions like, "Do you have a boyfriend?" or "Do you want to get married?" No, I don't have a boyfriend. Sometimes I want to get married. Most of the time I don't—I like being single. I've always wanted to have children, so I spend a lot of time with other people's children.

I edited this book. As I read it, I had the perspective of someone who's a little older than you probably are and who is asking different questions than you might be asking right now. I thought, *What about the girl who will never marry? What will she remember about this book several years from now? How will it help her?* I have a lot of friends who are single; some like being single, but many of them would rather be married. Some even wonder whether God likes them less because they're single. But some of God's favorite people in the Bible were single. Jeremiah, Daniel, and Paul were single, and so were Mary and Martha—and Jesus. Obviously, being single can be a good thing for some people. God hasn't just forgotten to find a husband for me; He has a special plan for me. He may give me a husband someday, or He may not. Either way, it's OK. It's probably hard for you to accept that idea quite as readily as I do, and that's OK too.

Some people think the worst part about being single is not having sex. That really isn't the most important part for me. Other than not having children, for me the hardest thing is probably that I don't have anyone to do the things that husbands do around the house, like taking care of the car (or buying a newer one) or changing light bulbs that are too high for me to reach. It would be nice if I had a husband who would hug me if I was depressed and if I could help a man become a more godly person, which is the main thing a wife is supposed to do. A husband should be a partner, and making decisions with someone else is easier than making them by oneself.

But a lot of things about my life wouldn't be as nice if I got married. My schedule is more flexible. I can be by myself whenever I want to. I don't have to worry about whether my husband likes my friends or whether I like his family. If I'm sick, I can stay in bed without having to get up and take care of kids. When I make something for supper that's really good, I have lots of leftovers, but I don't have to cook anything fancy if I don't want to. I've had several roommates, and, like me, all roommates have bad habits, but it would be harder to put up with a husband's bad habits. Scripture admits it's actually harder to be married than to be single (1 Corinthians 7:28b).

I decided a long time ago that it was OK to be single, and that if I ever got married, it would be to a really special man. Being married to him would have to be better than being single. Of course he would have to be a good Christian who cared about pleasing God, and he would have to be committed to marriage without the possibility of divorce. He would have to really like kids. He would need to have a good sense of humor, be intelligent, make enough money so I could stay home when we had children, and be someone I enjoyed being around. He would probably be a virgin, because that's really important to me. He would have to have the same standards, like not wanting to have a TV in the house when we had kids. He would have to really love me and be someone I could really respect.

I grew up hearing that I should stay a virgin because it was important to be a virgin when I got married. But I have found several reasons that it is important not to have sex with someone other than my husband even if I never get married. First, if I had sex, I wouldn't be as likely to still be happy single, so I might marry the wrong man just to have sex. Second, I wouldn't be a good example to the children I teach. Third, I might get a sexually transmitted disease or get pregnant, and I'd have the shame of having everyone know I had disobeyed God. Fourth, sex with someone who wasn't my husband wouldn't even be very special, and I'd get my heart broken badly when we broke up.

But none of those is the most important reason. God said not to—*that's* the most important reason. Do you want to know what was one of the most exciting reasons to me when I discovered it? In the Bible, the church is called the bride of Christ, and Revelation says the bride of Christ will someday be clothed in white wedding gowns (Revelation 3:4–5; 19:7–8). I'm engaged to be "married" to Christ, and He's perfect. I would want to be able to wear a white wedding gown if I ever got married. If I don't get married, I want Christ to be my only "husband," and I'm glad I'll still get to wear a white wedding dress someday.

The apostle Paul said that singleness can be very good (1 Corinthians 7:8, 32–35). He said that single people have opportunities to do more for God, because they don't have to take care of a husband or wife and children. Because I'm not busy with my own children, I have more time to teach Sunday school and do other things with children. I also can work at a full-time job. Some single people are missionaries in places where it's hard to raise children, or they do a lot of traveling.

Marriage was God's idea, and it's a really good one. For most people, marriage is better than singleness. But singleness is better than a bad marriage, and for some people singleness is best. God knows what is best for you, and He loves you enough to give it to you if you wait and let Him.

Love,
Cheryl Dunlop

Cheryl Dunlop is a General Editor at Moody Press. She lives on the West Side of Chicago, where she is actively involved with children in her church and opens her home to neighborhood children who come by to read, make craft projects, bake cookies, and talk.

A Special Letter on Abortion

Hello, Friend,

I want to invite you into one of the most private moments of my life. It was the moment my life was sliced in two, if you will. I say it was sliced into two because the person I was before this moment was drastically different from the person I quickly became for many years to come.

I was 19. I was the daughter of a pastor. I was attending a Christian college and dating the son of a pastor. I was having fun, enjoying both the newfound freedom of college and a really neat dating relationship with a Christian guy.

Sounds picture-perfect so far, right? Suddenly the unthinkable happened. I got pregnant. My boyfriend was less than supportive and seemed to threaten to turn my whole world upside down if I carried the pregnancy to term. He taunted me with stories of getting me kicked out of college. (The college expelled pregnant, unwed students.) He even relayed my own assessment—that my mother would probably have a mental breakdown. He convinced me that I didn't have much choice.

I aborted my baby. He would have graduated in 2000, and there isn't a day that goes by when I don't think about him.

I could have been engulfed in the most horrible grief imaginable, but I didn't have anyone to face it with me, and I wasn't willing to do it alone. I chose to numb myself. I drowned my feelings with drugs and promiscuity for many years. I just wanted to escape the overwhelming pain. And in many ways, I did. The only thing I believed during that time was that I made the right decision for that period of my life.

But one day, I found that there was no escaping it. I had to face it. While it was the most painful time in my life, grieving my child brought healing. Finding forgiveness from Christ furthered the journey that brought me to peace that passes all understanding. Then God gave me the inspiration that He could work even abortion to His good.

The world can debate abortion all it wants, but the fact remains there is pain.

I am so much happier now than I was when I was in denial and had convinced myself that I had only aborted a "blob of tissue." I am very loved by a wonderful husband, and I find tremendous fulfillment in a productive and successful career helping other women heal from abortion. The Lord has allowed me to rescue a few children who would have been aborted had their mothers not heard my testimony.

What do I tell these women? What do I see working as they seek to heal? First, I tell them that they are not alone. The Alan Guttmacher Institute (the research arm of Planned Parenthood, the world's largest abortion provider) recently stated that, "At the current rate, 43% of women will have at least one abortion by the time they are 45 years old."[1] And you might find this surprising, but women in the church are not immune. Imagine that 43% of all women are postabortive—they sit in your congregations, work in your schools, climb corporate ladders to success, and exist in every part of our society. Despite those statistics, abortion is rarely discussed by those who have chosen it.

Second, I would have to say that a good step toward healing can start with confession. Oh, I had confessed it before God, but confessing it to a loving, godly adult through sharing my testimony was a major step in my journey to healing. James 5:16 says, "Confess your sins to each other . . . so that you may be healed." God gave us each other to encourage and provide help in the process of healing. Telling this truth was one of the most frightening things I've ever done, but it was very worth it. I tell people to just make sure this person is one that they can trust.

I hope that you can't really identify with my story. I hope that you aren't hiding from the pain of abortion. I hope you can't feel the overwhelming grief. But if you can, let me encourage you to tell an older, wiser, and very godly woman. If you don't feel you can talk to your mom about it right now, find a local crisis pregnancy center to talk to one of their counselors—they can be found in the "Abortion Alternative" section of your Yellow Pages. I know that sounds tough, but it will be very worth it.

Speaking as someone who knows what premarital sex cost me, I can say that the best way to avoid pain is to remain abstinent until marriage. Your heart is very precious and should be saved for the perfect man. One of my greatest regrets is that I couldn't share my innocence with my husband. Regardless of the fact that the "sky doesn't fall" when you go a little bit further with your boyfriend than you would have liked, there are major consequences to your future. The boy who truly loves you will wait for marriage.

My prayer for you, if you have experienced abortion, is that you would join me in my journey. Never encourage or support a friend in making the choice to abort—regardless of their circumstances. Abortion is never the solution. It only makes matters worse by bringing more pain and regret into their hearts. Lead them to a crisis pregnancy center where they can find the truth about abortion and help to continue their pregnancy.

In God's Great Healing Love,
Sydna

Sydna Masse is the former director of Focus on the Family's Crisis Pregnancy outreach. She is now president and founder of Ramah International, Inc., a postabortion ministry (www.ramahinternational.org). She is the author of *Her Choice to Heal: Finding Spiritual and Emotional Peace After Abortion* (Chariot Victor). Her book tells her story in-depth and provides the opportunity for the reader to reflect on her own abortion situation and to begin the process of finding emotional and spiritual healing.

———— ⊰•⊱ ————

NOTE
1. "Facts in Brief—Induced Abortion," The Alan Guttmacher Institute, Washington, D.C., January 1997.

For information on Dannah's
"Seven Secrets to Sexual Purity"
retreats or speaking engagements,
or to purchase the retreat
curriculum that accompanies
And the Bride Wore White, write to

Pure Freedom,
attn: Kay Barker
360 Lightner St.
State College, PA 16803

*Moody Press, a ministry of
Moody Bible Institute, is designed
for education, evangelization, and
edification. If we may assist you in
knowing more about Christ and
the Christian life, please write us
without obligation:*

*Moody Press
c/o MLM
Chicago, IL 60610*